THE CHINESE
AND FAR EASTERN
COOKBOOK

THE CHINESE
AND FAR EASTERN
COOKBOOK

Ho Mei Yin

Exeter Books

NEW YORK

First published in Great Britain in 1984
by Ward Lock Limited, 82 Gower Street,
London WC1E 6EQ, a Pentos Company.

First published in USA 1984
by Exeter Books
Distributed by Bookthrift
Exeter is a trademark of Simon & Schuster, Inc.
Bookthrift is a registered trademark of Simon & Schuster, Inc.
New York, New York

ISBN 0-671-31166-2

Printed in Italy

CONTENTS

All recipes serve four people, unless otherwise specified.

Unusual ingredients may be purchased from Chinese groceries and other oriental food shops.

Soups

Basic Chinese Chicken Stock

3 pounds chicken, quartered
2 quarts water
1 small onion, chopped
3 stalks celery, chopped

1 small piece root ginger, crushed
1 tablespoon dry sherry
1 teaspoon salt

Place the chicken pieces in a large, heavy saucepan. Add the water and bring to the boil. Skim off any froth or bits which rise to the surface. Reduce the heat and simmer, covered, for 1½ hours.

Remove the chicken pieces from the pan and discard; all their flavor will have cooked out. Add the onion, celery and ginger to the stock and allow to stand for 20 minutes. Then add the sherry and salt and simmer for 10 minutes. Strain the stock through a clean cloth and leave to cool completely. Then skim off the fat which will have risen to the surface.

Basic Chinese Meat Stock

1 pound lean pork
½ pound chicken wings, carcass, giblets, etc.
2 quarts water
2 carrots, chopped

1 small onion, chopped
1 piece root ginger, crushed
1 teaspoon salt
2 teaspoons soy sauce

Place the pork and chicken in a large, heavy saucepan. Add the water and bring slowly to the boil. Skim off any froth or bits which rise to the surface. Reduce the heat and simmer, covered, for 20 minutes. Remove the pork and chicken from the pan; they can be kept for other dishes. Add the carrots, onion and ginger to the stock and simmer for 30 minutes. Add the salt and soy sauce and simmer for a further 5 minutes. Strain the stock through a clean cloth and leave to cool completely. Then skim off the fat which will have risen to the surface.

Wonton Soup

Serves 6

1 cup flour	¼ pound ground pork
salt	2 teaspoons soy sauce
1 egg	ground ginger
1 tablespoon milk	2 quarts chicken stock (see
2 tablespoons oil	page 7)
¼ pound spinach, washed and picked over	1 tablespoon chopped chives

Wontons are small, stuffed pastry parcels; they are usually eaten as an accompaniment to soup.

To make the wontons, sieve the flour and a pinch of salt into a bowl. Break in the egg and add the milk and oil. Mix to a firm but pliant dough. Roll out very thinly on a lightly floured surface. Cut into 3 inch squares. Cover with a cloth while preparing the stuffing.

To make the stuffing, put the spinach into a bowl, pour boiling water over and leave for 3 minutes. Drain well and chop. Put the pork in a bowl and stir in the soy sauce and a pinch ground ginger. Add the spinach and mix.

Put 1 teaspoon of stuffing in the center of each pastry square. Fold over one side of the pastry to form a roll, pressing to seal the long edge. Fold the two ends of pastry at the ends of the roll over each other and press together. Bring the stock to the boil in a large saucepan. Add the wontons and simmer, covered, for 20 minutes. Divide the wontons into soup bowls and pour the stock over them. Sprinkle with chives and serve.

Chinese Pork and Bean Sprout Soup

¾ ounce dried Chinese mushrooms	5 ounces canned bean sprouts, drained
2 ounces transparent noodles	2 quarts hot chicken stock (see
¾ pound lean pork	page 7)
4 tablespoons oil	salt, pepper
1 onion, chopped	2 tablespoons soy sauce
1 clove garlic, chopped	sugar

Soak the mushrooms in warm water for 15 to 30 minutes, until swollen. Cut the noodles into 4 inch lengths. Put them into a bowl and cover with boiling salted water. Allow to stand for 5 minutes. Drain, rinse with cold water and drain again. Drain the mushrooms, and halve or quarter them if large. While the mushrooms and noodles are soaking, cut the pork into narrow strips.

Heat the oil in a skillet and fry the pork on all sides for 5 minutes. Remove and keep hot. Fry the onion and garlic in the pan for 3 minutes, until just soft. Put the pork back in the pan, and add the bean sprouts, noodles, mushrooms and stock. Season with salt, pepper, the soy sauce and a pinch sugar. Bring to the boil and simmer for 8 minutes. Serve in warmed soup bowls.

CHINESE NOODLE SOUP

Serves 6

½ pound boned leg of pork
2 tablespoons Chinese rice
  wine or dry sherry
2 tablespoons soy sauce
salt, pepper, ground ginger
⅓ ounce dried Chinese
  mushrooms
5 ounces canned bamboo
  shoots, drained

¼ pound canned chicken,
  drained
¼ pound cooked ham, sliced
½ pound Chinese noodles
2 quarts chicken stock (see
  page 7)
oil for frying
sprigs cress

Cut the pork into small strips. Mix the rice wine or sherry, soy sauce and seasonings to taste in a bowl. Add the pork, cover and leave to marinate for 1 hour. After 30 minutes put the mushrooms to soak in warm water for 15 to 30 minutes, until swollen. Meanwhile prepare the other ingredients. Cut the bamboo shoots into thin strips and cut the chicken into 1 inch cubes. Trim any fat from the ham and cut into 1 inch squares. Bring a pan of salted water to the boil. Add the noodles and simmer for 10 minutes. Drain in a sieve, rinse in cold water and drain again. Drain the mushrooms.

Put the stock, mushrooms, bamboo shoots and noodles into a large saucepan. Heat gently for 3 minutes. Meanwhile take the pork out of the marinade and drain. Heat the oil in a skillet and fry the pork strips on all sides for 2 minutes. Remove and add to the soup with the chicken and ham pieces. Heat through gently. Pour the soup into warmed soup bowls, sprinkle with cress and serve.

Chinese Noodle Soup

CHINESE ASPARAGUS SOUP

1 quart chicken stock (see
  page 7)
¼ pound leeks, sliced
1 clove garlic
salt, pepper, ground ginger,
  curry powder

1 tablespoon shortening
2 tablespoons soy sauce
6 ounces canned crabmeat,
  drained
½ pound canned asparagus
  spears, drained.

Bring the chicken stock to the boil in a large saucepan, add the leeks and simmer for 20 minutes. Crush the garlic with salt. Melt the dripping in another pan and fry the garlic until golden. Add to the soup. Then add the soy sauce and seasonings to taste. Remove any hard pieces from the crabmeat, flake it and add to the soup. Add the asparagus spears, then heat them in the soup. Adjust seasoning and serve.

CHINESE VEGETABLE SOUP

½ pound lean pork
5 tablespoons soy sauce
2 teaspoons flour
salt, pepper, ground ginger
2 carrots
¼ pound canned bamboo
  shoots, drained
2 ounces spinach, washed and
  picked over

2 tablespoons oil
1½ quarts hot stock
2 ounces fresh mushrooms,
  thinly sliced
½ ounce transparent noodles
2 tablespoons Chinese rice
  wine or dry sherry

Cut the pork into narrow strips. Mix 2 tablespoons soy sauce with the flour in a cup. Season to taste with salt and pepper. Put the meat in a bowl, spoon the marinade over it, cover and leave to stand for 10 minutes. Meanwhile cut the carrots and bamboo shoots into thin strips. Cut the spinach leaves through once.

Heat the oil in a large saucepan. Remove the meat from the marinade, drain and fry in the oil, on all sides, for 10 minutes. Add the stock to the pan with the carrots and simmer for another 10 minutes. Add the bamboo shoots, mushrooms and noodles and simmer for a further 10 minutes, until just tender. Five minutes before the end of the cooking time add the spinach leaves. Season to taste with the remaining soy sauce, the rice wine or sherry, ginger and salt. Serve at once in warmed soup bowls.

KIEMBLO

1 slice wholewheat bread,
  crusts removed
½ pound hamburger
salt, pepper
1½ quarts stock
1 tablespoon oil
1 onion, sliced
¼ pound cabbage, chopped

1 leek sliced,
2 ounces fresh mushrooms,
  sliced
6 ounces celery, sliced
2 ounces frozen peas
¼ pound ribbon noodles
1 tablespoon soy sauce
3 tablespoons Chinese rice
  wine or dry sherry

Soak the bread in a little water and squeeze out the excess. Mix the beef and bread together and season to taste. Shape into small oval dumplings with a teaspoon. Bring the stock to the boil in a pan, put in the dumplings, and simmer for 10 minutes. Meanwhile heat the oil in a large saucepan, add the onion, and fry for 3 minutes until pale brown. Add the cabbage, leek, mushrooms and celery and fry for another 5 minutes. Take the dumplings out of the stock, drain and keep warm. Strain the stock on to the vegetable mixture. Add the peas and noodles and simmer for 15 minutes, until the peas and noodles are done. Put the dumplings back into the soup, add the soy sauce and rice wine or sherry, and season to taste. Serve at once.

PEKING HOT-SOUR SOUP

⅓ ounce dried Chinese
  mushrooms
¼ pound lean pork
1 piece bamboo (fresh or
  canned)
½ pad bean curd
1 egg
water to mix
1 tablespoon cornstarch

1 quart chicken stock (see
  page 7)
2 tablespoons white vinegar
1½ tablespoons soy sauce
salt, pepper
½ teaspoon sesame oil
1 tablespoon chopped chives
  or 1 chopped scallion
  (optional)

Soak the mushrooms in warm water for 15 to 30 minutes, until swollen. Drain, remove the stems, and cut the caps into thin strips. Cut the pork and bamboo into thin strips, and the bean curd into slightly thicker strips. Beat the egg in a bowl with 1 teaspoon water. Mix the cornstarch to a smooth paste with 4 tablespoons water.

Bring the stock to the boil in a large saucepan, add the meat and mushrooms, and simmer for 8 minutes. Add the bamboo and bean curd and simmer for a further 4 minutes. Stir in the vinegar and soy sauce and season to taste. Bring to the boil and stir in the egg. When the egg has set in swirls, stir in the cornstarch paste until the soup binds and becomes clear and glossy. Then stir in the oil. Serve in warmed soup bowls and sprinkle with chopped chives or scallion if desired.

INDONESIAN CHICKEN SOUP

salt, pepper
2 quarts water
3 pounds chicken
1 small onion, sliced
1 tablespoon ground ginger
7 ounces canned bean sprouts,
  drained

½ pound canned celery,
  drained and chopped
½ cup sherry
soy sauce
4 hard-cooked eggs, chopped
1 tablespoon chopped chives

Add salt to the water and bring to the boil in a large pan. Put in the chicken, cover and simmer for 1 hour, or until tender.

Remove the chicken from the stock and put aside. Then add to the stock the onion, garlic, ginger, and pepper to taste. Simmer for 15 minutes. Meanwhile remove the skin from the chicken, take the meat off the bones and cut into small, even sized pieces. Keep warm. Mix the bean sprouts and celery in a bowl with the sherry. Season to taste with soy sauce. Put the chicken pieces into a warmed soup tureen, add the vegetables and eggs, and pour the stock on top. Sprinkle with chives and serve.

STARTERS, SAUCES AND SIDE DISHES

PEACOCK PLATTER

The peacock platter is a cold Chinese hors d'oeuvre consisting of thinly sliced meats and other ingredients, and it is served on special occasions. If prepared and arranged with care, the dish looks like the outspread tail of a displaying peacock. It is impossible to give an exact recipe: it can be as simple or as elaborate as you like. Among possible ingredients are: boiled or steamed chicken, red-cooked meat or poultry, ham and abalone. All ingredients are very thinly sliced and then arranged in the form of a fan on a plate.

As can be seen from the picture, slices of hard-cooked eggs, decorated with red and green maraschino cherries, can be used to represent the eyes of the peacock. Other decoration can be provided by figures cut out of carrots or radishes. Asparagus, cucumber slices, radish roses, pieces of pineapple, and anything else you like can be used to decorate the peacock's tail. Hoisin and plum sauce can be served as dips, and can be bought ready-prepared from oriental groceries.

SWEET-AND-SOUR SAUCE

3 tablespoons corn starch	1 green pepper, seeded and finely chopped
¼ cup water	
2 tablespoons soft brown sugar	1 large, firm tomato, skinned, seeded and finely chopped
½ cup red wine	
3 tablespoons tomato catsup	3 slices canned pineapple, drained and finely chopped
1 tablespoon soy sauce	
1 teaspoon mustard powder	salt, pepper

Mix together the cornstarch and water in a pan until smooth. Add the sugar, wine, tomato catsup, soy sauce and mustard powder. Bring slowly to the boil, stirring continuously. Boil for 2 minutes, until the sauce turns clear. Then add the pepper, tomato and pineapple. Bring the sauce back to the boil and adjust seasoning to taste. Serve in a warmed sauceboat.

Peacock Platter

Spring Rolls

½ pound flour
1½ cups water
1½ teaspoons coconut oil
salt, cayenne
4 tablespoons oil
¼ pound ground pork
¼ pound hamburger
½ pound white cabbage or
 Chinese cabbage, cut into
 thin strips
1 leek, cut into thin strips
1 onion, finely chopped

½ pound canned bamboo
 shoots, drained and cut into
 thin strips
¼ pound canned mushrooms,
 drained and chopped
7 ounces canned bean sprouts,
 drained
4 tablespoons soy sauce
4 tablespoons Chinese rice
 wine or dry sherry
coconut oil for frying
1 egg yolk, beaten
oil for deep frying

First make the batter. Place the flour in a bowl and gradually stir in the water, stirring in the same direction all the time. Stir in the 1½ teaspoons coconut oil and a pinch salt. Cover and leave to stand for 30 minutes.

To prepare the stuffing, heat the 4 tablespoons oil in a pan. Add the ground meats and fry for 2 minutes, stirring. Add the strips of cabbage and leek, the onion and the bamboo shoots, and fry gently for 5 minutes. Add the mushrooms and bean sprouts, and stew for a further 2 minutes. Season with the soy sauce, rice wine or sherry, salt and cayenne. Set aside.

Lightly paint the surface of a large skillet with coconut oil. Pour in an eighth of the batter, spread it out evenly by tilting the pan, and cook over a very gentle heat until firm and lightly browned on both sides. Make 7 other crepes in the same way, placing them between damp cloths when cooked.

Cut the 8 crepes into 8 large squares. Divide the stuffing between the crepes, spreading it out on the surface. Fold two opposite corners towards the middle. Starting with one of the other corners (the one nearest to you) roll up the pancake. Paint the last corner with beaten egg yolk and press the roll well together. Heat the oil to a temperature of 350°F and deep fry the spring rolls. Take them out, drain on absorbent paper and serve on a warmed plate.

Siu Pai Quat

2 pounds spare ribs
1 teaspoon salt
1 teaspoon sugar
1 clove garlic, crushed
1 teaspoon chopped root
 ginger

3 tablespoons soy sauce
1 tablespoon sake, Chinese
 rice wine or dry sherry
2 tablespoons hoisin sauce
2 tablespoons honey

You need very short ribs for this recipe, only about 4–5½ inches long and not too meaty. Cut down through the meat, about halfway between the ribs.

Rub the ribs with the salt and sugar and leave for 1 hour. Pound and mash together the garlic and ginger, and mix with the soy sauce, sake (or rice wine or sherry), hoisin sauce and honey. Marinate the meat in this mixture for 3 hours, turning regularly.

Drain the ribs, reserving the marinade. Place the ribs on a rack in a roasting pan containing water, and bake for 1 hour at 325–375°F. Then turn the oven up to maximum heat and bake the ribs for a further 5 to 10 minutes. Remove from the oven, separate the ribs with a knife and serve as an hors d'oeuvre to a Chinese meal, accompanied by scallion tassels (see page 76).

SAMBAL BAJAK

8-10 red chilli peppers, seeded and finely chopped
4-6 red onions, chopped or 2-3 small onions, chopped
2 cloves garlic, crushed
8 blanched almonds, crushed
1 teaspoon belacan (prawn paste)
1 tablespoon soft brown sugar
1 teaspoon salt
2 tablespoons oil
2 tablespoons tamarind pulp, chopped
1 bay leaf
2 tablespoons water

Thoroughly pound and mash together the chillies, onions, garlic, nuts, belacan (prawn paste), sugar and salt. Heat the oil in a heavy-based skillet and fry the spice mixture in it for 2 to 3 minutes. Add the tamarind, bay leaf and water, and continue simmering over medium heat until all the oil has been absorbed. Stir continuously to prevent sticking, especially as the ingredients become drier. Remove the bay leaf, let the sambal cool to room temperature, and then transfer to a clean glass jar. Store the sambal, with the jar tightly stoppered, in the refrigerator.

SAMBAL TAOCO

8-10 red chilli peppers, seeded and finely chopped
3-4 red onions, chopped or 1 large onion, chopped
3 cloves garlic, crushed
½ teaspoon belacan (prawn paste)
1 teaspoon galingale (optional)
1 teaspoon soft brown sugar
2-3 tablespoons oil
3-4 tablespoons soy-bean paste
1 tablespoon tamarind pulp, chopped
3-4 tablespoons water

Thoroughly pound and mash together the chillies, onions, garlic, belacan (prawn paste), galingale and sugar. Heat the oil in a heavy-based skillet, add the spice mixture and fry for 2 to 3 minutes. Add the soy-bean paste, tamarind and water and simmer gently until all the oil has been absorbed. Let the sambal cool to room temperature, and then transfer to a clean glass jar. Store the sambal, with the jar tightly stoppered, in the refrigerator.

SAMBAL GORENG TELUR

3 red chilli peppers, chopped
4 red onions, chopped
2 cloves garlic, crushed
½ teaspoon belacan (prawn paste)
2 teaspoons galingale (optional)
2½ teaspoons soft brown sugar
1 tablespoon tamarind pulp, chopped
salt
2 tablespoons oil
1 cup coconut milk
2 bay leaves
4 hard-cooked eggs

Pound and mash together the chillies, onions, garlic, belacan (prawn paste), galingale, brown sugar and tamarind. Season to taste with salt. Heat the oil in a heavy-based skillet, add the mashed ingredients and fry gently for 2 to 3 minutes. Add the coconut milk and bay leaves, stir, and simmer for a few minutes. Add the eggs and simmer gently, stirring occasionally, until the oil separates from the sauce. Remove the eggs from the pan, let them cool a little, and halve them lengthways. Place them on a bowl with the rounded side uppermost. Pour the sauce over and serve immediately as a hot side dish with a Malaysian or Indonesian-style dinner.

SAMBAL GORENG HATI

9 ounces calves' liver
1 small onion, chopped
1 clove garlic, crushed
1½ teaspoons chilli sauce
1 teaspoon galingale
  (optional)
1 teaspoon soft brown sugar

½ teaspoon belacan (prawn
  paste)
1 teaspoon salt
3 tablespoons oil
1 tablespoon tamarind pulp,
  chopped
1 cup coconut milk

Soak the liver in cold water for 15 minutes. Remove from the water, pat dry with absorbent paper, and cut into short, thin strips. Pound and mash together the onion, garlic, chilli sauce, galingale, sugar, belacan (prawn paste) and salt. Heat the oil in a heavy-based skillet and fry the mixture. Add the liver and continue frying over medium heat, turning occasionally, until the liver starts to brown. Add the tamarind and stir for 1 minute. Pour in the coconut milk and allow to simmer for 5 minutes, or until the liver is done. Serve as a side dish with a Malaysian or Indonesian-style meal.

REMPEYEK IKAN TERI

1 ounce dried ikan teri or
  1 ounce canned anchovies
2 cloves garlic, crushed
½ teaspoon ground coriander
½ teaspoon turmeric

3 blanched almonds, mashed
salt
3–5 tablespoons coconut milk
1 cup rice flour
oil for frying

Ikan teri are tiny, anchovy-like dried fish that can be eaten whole, although some people prefer to snap the heads off first. These dried fish are sold in oriental groceries, sometimes curried. When the fish are to be fried, as in this recipe, it is advisable to dry them out a little more, either in the sun, or indoors near the fire or a radiator. (Canned anchovies will, of course, need drying completely.)

Pound and mash together the garlic, coriander, turmeric, nuts and a pinch salt. Stir sufficient coconut milk into the flour to make a smooth batter, not too thin. Stir the fish and the spice mixture into the batter, and leave to stand for 10 minutes. Heat a film of oil in a wok or skillet. Stir the batter again, put a spoonful into the skillet and tip so that it quickly spreads to cover the base of the skillet. Fry to a golden brown on both sides, remove from the pan and drain on absorbent paper. Keep warm. Continue until all the batter has been cooked. Serve as a side dish with a Malaysian or Indonesian-style meal.

Rempeyek Ikan Teri

FISH AND SHELLFISH

STEAMED SEA BASS

1 sea bass or other firm-
fleshed sea fish, cleaned and
  scaled
1 teaspoon salt
2 teaspoons oil
1 leek
1 small piece root ginger,
  peeled and finely chopped
1½ tablespoons sake, Chinese
  rice wine or dry sherry
1 tablespoon soy sauce
½ teaspoon sugar
8 scallion tassels (see page 76)

Do not remove the head and tail when cleaning the fish. Wash the cleaned fish under the cold tap and pat dry with absorbent paper. Make a few, shallow, diagonal cuts on either side of the fish. Rub in the salt and then the oil. Place the fish on its side in a casserole just large enough for it. Cut the leek into 2 inch strips. Cover the fish with the leek and the chopped ginger. Mix the sake (or rice wine, or sherry), soy sauce and sugar, and stir until the sugar has dissolved. Pour this sauce over the fish and place the dish in a large steamer. Steam for 30 to 40 minutes. Remove the dish from the steamer, arrange the scallion tassels around the fish, and serve at once.

SOUTH SEAS FISH

Serves 5

5 cod steaks (½ pound each)
½ cup lemon juice
salt, pepper, ground mace,
  powdered saffron
3 tablespoons butter
2 onions, chopped
2 cups water
1 teaspoon ginger syrup (from
  jar preserved stem ginger)
grated rind 2 lemons
3 tablespoons flour
4 eggs, beaten
1 teaspoon chopped parsley

Rinse the fish under cold water and pat dry with absorbent paper. Sprinkle with 1½ tablespoons lemon juice and allow to stand for 10 minutes. Season the fish with salt and pepper. Melt the butter in a large skillet and fry the onions until soft. Then add the fish steaks and brown on all sides for 5 minutes. Add the water, ginger syrup, lemon rind, remaining lemon juice and a pinch mace, and bring to the boil. Simmer over low heat for 10 minutes.

Meanwhile, stir the flour into the eggs, and season with saffron. Add a little of the liquid from the fish, and season with more salt if necessary. Stir in the parsley. Pour the mixture over the fish. Stirring carefully, bring the contents of the pan to just below boiling point. Take the pan off the heat, arrange the fish in a serving bowl, pour on the sauce, and serve at once.

JAPANESE FISH IN SWEET-AND-SOUR SAUCE

1 pound fillets of white fish
juice ½ lemon
5 tablespoons soy sauce
salt
2 tablespoons potato flour
5 tablespoons vinegar
½ cup water
2 tablespoons sugar
3 slices lemon
oil for deep frying
2 tablespoons cornstarch

Wash the fish fillets under the cold tap and pat dry with absorbent paper. Put them in a bowl and trickle the lemon juice over. Add 2 tablespoons soy sauce. Turn the fish in the marinade, then cut into strips 1¼ inches wide. Leave to marinate for 15 minutes. Season with salt and toss in the potato flour. Form the strips of fish into sausage shapes with your hands.

To make the sauce, put the vinegar, water, sugar, remaining soy sauce and the lemon slices in a pan. Bring to the boil, then reduce the heat and simmer very gently for 20 minutes. Meanwhile, deep fry the fish in the oil for about 8 minutes. Remove from the oil, drain on absorbent paper and keep warm. Finally, thicken the sauce. Mix the cornstarch to a smooth paste in a cup with a little cold water. Blend a little of the hot sauce into the mixture, then return to the pan. Bring slowly to the boil, stirring constantly. Simmer for 2 to 3 minutes to allow the flour to cook through.

To serve, arrange the fish on a warmed plate. The sauce can either be poured over, or served separately in a jug.

CHINESE FISH

1 trout (1 pound), cleaned
1 carp (3 pounds), cleaned and scaled
juice 1½ lemons
salt, pepper, ground star anise
2 ounces smoked ham
1 pound fresh mushrooms, sliced
2 pieces, preserved stem ginger, sliced
3 tablespoons soy sauce
1 cup hot water
4 large cabbage leaves
2 teaspoons cornstarch
2 tablespoons shortening
1 tablespoon chopped parsley
1 lemon, cut into slices

Wash both fish under the cold tap and pat dry with absorbent paper. Season inside and out with the juice 1 lemon. Make several cuts across the backs of both fish. Rub in salt and pepper. Cut the ham into thin strips and insert into the cuts. Grease an oval casserole and put the fish in it. Mix together the mushrooms and ginger and scatter over the fish. Pour the soy sauce over and sprinkle with a pinch ground star anise. Add a little of the hot water, cover and place in the oven. Bake for 30 minutes at 400°F.

While the fish is baking add the rest of the hot water gradually. Baste the fish from time to time with the cooking liquid. Remove when cooked and arrange on the cabbage leaves in a warmed bowl. Keep warm.

Stir the fish juices from the casserole with a little cold water and bring to the boil. To thicken the sauce, mix the cornstarch to a smooth paste in a cup with a little cold water. Blend a little of the hot liquid into the mixture, then return to the casserole. Bring slowly to the boil, stirring constantly. Simmer for 2 to 3 minutes to allow the flour to cook through. Pour into a sauce boat to serve separately and keep warm. Finally heat the shortening in a small pan. Pour over the fish with the juice ½ lemon. Garnish with the parsley and lemon slices and serve with the sauce.

ORIENTAL FISH WITH GRAPEFRUIT

1½ pounds fillet of cod	COURT BOUILLON
1 grapefruit, halved	1 onion
2 tablespoons butter	1 bay leaf
1 small onion, chopped	4 cloves
¼ cup flour	1 quart water
1 cup heavy cream	3 tablespoons white wine
salt, pepper, ground ginger	vinegar
2 hard-cooked eggs, chopped	1 teaspoon salt
	4 peppercorns

Divide the cod fillet into four pieces. Wash the fish under the cold tap and pat dry with absorbent paper. To make the court bouillon, peel the onion and make several deep cuts in it. Insert the bay leaf and cloves into the cuts. Bring the water, vinegar and salt to the boil in a large pan, then add the onion and peppercorns. Add the fish to the pan and poach gently for 15 minutes, until done. Meanwhile squeeze the juice from one grapefruit half. Divide the other half into segments, remove pith and skin, chop coarsely and set aside. Remove the fish from the court bouillon and keep warm. Reserve 1 cup of the liquid.

Melt the butter in a skillet. Fry the onion for 5 minutes, until golden. Scatter in the flour and simmer for 3 minutes, stirring. Add the reserved court bouillon and bring to the boil, still stirring. Simmer for 8 minutes. Stir in the cream and grapefruit juice. Put the sauce through a strainer. Season to taste with salt, pepper and a pinch ground ginger. Arrange the fish on a warmed serving plate, pour the sauce over, and garnish with the eggs and grapefruit pieces. Serve at once.

SINGAPORE FISH WITH CURRY SAUCE

4 halibut steaks (½ pound each)	3 tablespoons flour
juice 1½ lemons	½ cup water
½ cup stock	3 tablespoons apple purée
½ cup white wine	1 teaspoon sugar
1 bay leaf	½ pound canned mushrooms, drained
salt, pepper	1 banana
⅓ cup butter	
3 tablespoons curry powder	

Pat the halibut steaks dry with absorbent paper and sprinkle them with the juice of 1 lemon. Bring the stock and wine to the boil in a large saucepan. Add the bay leaf and salt, and carefully put the fish into the pan. Poach for 10 minutes, until just cooked. Remove the fish from the pan, drain, and arrange on a warmed serving plate. Keep hot. Strain and reserve the fish stock in the pan.

To make the curry sauce, melt 3 tablespoons of the butter in a pan, add the curry powder and flour, and cook gently for 3 minutes. Pour the reserved fish stock and the water into the pan, stirring. Bring to the boil and simmer for 5 minutes. Then stir in the apple purée, and season the sauce with the remaining lemon juice, salt, pepper and the sugar. Reheat gently without boiling.

Melt 2 tablespoons of the butter in a skillet, and fry the mushrooms for 5 minutes. Season with salt and pepper, remove and keep hot. Peel the banana, cut it in half widthways, then cut each piece in half lengthways. Melt the remaining butter in another skillet and fry the banana pieces for 2 minutes each side, until golden. To serve, arrange the mushrooms on top of the halibut steaks, garnish with the banana pieces, and pour the sauce around the fish.

ORIENTAL FISH KABOBS

2 pounds fillets of mullet
4 small onions, halved
8 small tomatoes, halved
4 tablespoons olive oil
2 tablespoons sherry
1 teaspoon sugar
salt, pepper

MARINADE
1 clove garlic
salt
juice 2 lemons

SAUCE
1 cup yogurt
½ cup sour cream
1 teaspoon chopped parsley
1 teaspoon chopped chives
salt

These fish kabobs taste best broiled over charcoal, but an ordinary gas or electric broiler will still produce good results. Wash the mullet fillets under the cold tap and pat dry with absorbent paper. Cut into slices ½ inch thick, across the grain of the flesh. To make the marinade: crush the garlic with salt and mix in a bowl with the lemon juice. Add the fish slices and marinate for 15 minutes, turning frequently.

Meanwhile bring a pan of water to the boil and briefly blanch the onion halves. Drain the fish slices and roll them up. Place alternate rolls of fish, tomato and onion on skewers. Mix the oil, sherry, sugar, and salt and pepper to taste with 2 tablespoons of the marinade. Brush the kabobs with this mixture. Put them on a rack under the broiler, with the broiler pan below to catch the drips. Grill for 10 minutes, turning frequently, and brushing with the oil, sherry and marinade mixture.

While the kabobs are grilling, prepare the sauce. Beat the yogurt and cream together in a bowl until foamy. Add the parsley and chives and season with salt. Hand the kabobs and sauce separately.

Oriental Fish Kabobs

FISH IN SOY SAUCE

1 haddock, cod or mullet
  (2 pounds), cleaned
juice 1 lemon
½ pound pork fillet, thinly
  sliced
flour for coating
1 leek
⅓ cup oil
1 piece preserved stem ginger,
  sliced
¼ pound canned bamboo
  shoots, drained and sliced
5 ounces canned mushrooms,
  drained.

FISH MARINADE
1 tablespoon soy sauce
1 tablespoon Chinese rice
  wine or dry sherry
salt, pepper, ground ginger

MEAT MARINADE
1 tablespoon soy sauce
1 tablespoon Chinese rice
  wine or dry sherry
1 teaspoon flour

SAUCE
2 tablespoons Chinese rice
  wine or dry sherry
2 tablespoons soy sauce
sugar
salt
½ cup stock

Cut the head off the fish. Wash the fish under the cold tap and pat dry with absorbent paper. Trickle the lemon juice over it and leave to stand. Mix the ingredients for the fish marinade in a jug. Slash the fish several times across the backbone, put in a bowl, pour over the marinade and leave to stand for 30 minutes. Meanwhile coat the pork slices in flour. Mix the ingredients for the meat marinade in a bowl, add the pork and turn from time to time. To make the sauce: mix the rice wine or sherry, soy sauce and a pinch each sugar and salt in a bowl. Add the stock and keep aside. Then cut the leek into strips.

Remove the fish and pork from their marinades and drain. Heat the oil in a skillet large enough to take the fish. Add the ginger and leek and fry, stirring, for 5 minutes. Remove from the pan and keep warm. Put the fish in the skillet and brown on both sides (2 minutes each side). Add the bamboo shoots, pork and mushrooms, and return the leek and ginger to the pan. Pour the sauce over the fish and vegetables. Cover the pan and bring the contents to boiling point. Then reduce the heat and simmer for 15 minutes, until the fish is done. Transfer to a warmed bowl and serve.

JAPANESE SALAD

Serves 6

salt, paprika
1 cucumber, grated
2 carrots, grated
1 large white Japanese radish,
  grated
¼ pound fresh mushrooms,
  sliced
¾ pound crawfish tails,
  halved
1 tablespoon chopped parsley
1 tablespoon chopped borage
1 tablespoon chopped dill

2 eggs
sugar
¼ cup butter, melted
2 tablespoons white wine
  vinegar
1 peach, sliced
1 mandarin orange, divided
  into segments, pith and skin
  removed
½ orange, sliced

Sprinkle salt over the grated vegetables and leave for 30 minutes; pour off the liquid that will have been drawn. Then mix the vegetables with the mushrooms. Add the crawfish tails and herbs. Mix and leave to stand for 15 minutes. Meanwhile make the dressing. Beat together the eggs, a pinch each salt and sugar, and the butter in a heatproof bowl over a pan of hot water until foamy. Remove the bowl from the heat and gradually stir in the vinegar. Continue stirring until the sauce is cold. Season to taste with paprika. Arrange the grated vegetable mixture in a bowl and pour the sauce over the salad. Garnish with the peach, mandarin and orange slices.

MALAYSIAN FISH CURRY

1¾ pounds fillets of firm white
  fish
2 tablespoons lemon juice
salt, ground ginger
2 tablespoons curry powder
flour for coating

4 tablespoons coconut oil
butter for frying
3 onions, sliced
4 tablespoons milk
½ cup peanuts, halved
½ cup heavy cream

Wash the fish under the cold tap and pat dry with absorbent paper. Cut into 1½ inch cubes and place on a dish. Trickle the lemon juice over the fish, cover and allow to stand for 10 minutes.

Sprinkle salt and half the curry powder over the fish and coat with flour. Heat the oil in a large skillet and fry the fish cubes on all sides for 3 minutes, until light brown. Transfer to a serving bowl and keep warm. Melt the butter in another pan. Dip the onion rings in milk, then in flour, and fry in the hot fat for 5 minutes, until golden brown. Remove, drain and place over the fish cubes. Add the peanuts to the coconut oil in which the fish was cooked with a pinch each salt and ground ginger, the cream and remaining curry powder. Simmer gently for 2 minutes over low heat. Pour over the fish and serve.

KYOTO FISH FILLETS

2 pounds fillets of firm white
  fish
½ cup sake
½ cup oil
3 tablespoons sweet rice wine
  or sweet sherry

6 egg yolks, beaten
salt
sugar

Rinse the fish under cold water, pat dry with absorbent paper, and cut into cubes. Place the cubes in a bowl. Pour the sake over them, cover the bowl and allow to stand for 30 minutes. Take out the fish, drain and pat dry. Heat the oil in a large skillet. Add the fish and fry on all sides for 10 minutes, until just cooked.

Beat the sweet rice wine or sherry into the egg yolks, and season generously with salt and sugar. Pour this mixture over the fish, and cook gently for 3 minutes to allow the egg mixture to thicken. Transfer to a warmed bowl and serve at once.

SATE UDANG

1 pound large frozen shrimp,
  thawed
½ tablespoon soy sauce

½ teaspoon chilli sauce
1 teaspoon grated root ginger
1 teaspoon lemon juice

Cut the shrimp in half lengthways. Remove the black intestinal veins if necessary and then halve them again crossways. Thoroughly mix together the remaining ingredients, add the shrimp and leave to marinate for 30 minutes. Then thread the quartered shrimp on to skewers and grill over a barbeque until cooked. Pour the liquid from the marinade over them and serve.

SAMBAL GORENG UDANG

1 small onion, chopped
1 clove garlic, crushed
1 teaspoon ground ginger
1 teaspoon brown sugar
½ teaspoon belacan (shrimp paste)
1½ teaspoons chilli sauce
2 tablespoons oil
10 peteh beans (see note below)
1 tablespoon tamarind pulp, chopped
½ pound shrimp
1 bay leaf
½ cup coconut milk

Pound and mash together the onion, garlic, ginger, sugar, belacan (shrimp paste), and chilli sauce. Heat the oil in a heavy-based skillet and start to fry the mashed ingredients. Add the beans and tamarind, stir, and continue to fry for 1 minute. Stir in the shrimps and fry briefly. Add the bay leaf and coconut milk and simmer for a few minutes. Serve as a side dish.

Note Peteh beans are an almond-shaped variety sold in three forms: fresh, dried, or as a kind of light pickle. The fresh beans are still in their large green pods. The dried beans have a dark brown skin that can be removed after soaking for 30 minutes in warm water. If the pickled beans are bought, their skin will generally have been removed, and the beans are a yellowish-green colour; they only need rinsing before use. As peteh beans can be difficult to obtain, they may be omitted from the recipe if unobtainable.

TEMPURA

½ pound canned bamboo shoots, drained
2 sweet red peppers, seeded
2 green peppers, seeded
4 onions, sliced
1 pound frozen shrimp, thawed
2 pieces preserved stem ginger, sliced
1 cup flour
½ cup rice powder
8 egg whites
1 cup water
½ cup Chinese rice wine or dry sherry
oil for deep frying

Cut the bamboo shoots into rounds ½ inch thick, and cut the peppers into strips. Arrange the bamboo shoots, peppers, onions, shrimp and ginger in separate small bowls. Put the flour and rice powder into a bowl. Beat the egg whites with the water and rice wine or sherry. Stir gradually into the flour until you have a fairly liquid batter. Heat the oil in a fondue pot on the stove until it reaches a temperature of 350°F. Then put the fondue pot over its own burner.

Using a fondue fork, each guest dips his own ingredients in the batter and then deep fries them in the hot oil. Serve individual bowls of boiled rice, with a raw egg yolk broken over the top of each bowl, with this recipe. Hand soy sauce and grated white Japanese radish or horseradish in separate bowls as additional seasoning.

Sambal Goreng Udang

CURRIED SHRIMP

5 ounces canned bamboo
  shoots
1/3 ounce dried Chinese
  mushrooms
1/2 pound frozen snow peas
1 pound frozen shrimp,
  thawed
juice 1 lemon
1 egg white
3 tablespoons cornstarch
oil for deep frying

2 onions, chopped
ground ginger
1 green pepper, seeded and
  chopped
2 teaspoons curry powder
1 teaspoon sugar
2 tablespoons soy sauce
2 tablespoons Chinese rice
  wine or dry sherry

Drain the bamboo shoots, reserving the liquid. Cut the shoots into thin strips. Break the mushrooms into small pieces. Soak them in warm water for 15 to 30 minutes until swollen, and then drain. Meanwhile simmer the peas (still frozen) in a little water for 10 minutes, until tender. Drain and keep warm. Pat the shrimp dry with absorbent paper. Trickle lemon juice over them Beat the egg white and cornstarch together, dip the shrimp into this batter, and deep fry them in the oil for 2 or 3 minutes. Drain on absorbent paper and keep warm.

Heat 2 tablespoons of the frying oil in a skillet. Add the onions and bamboo shoots and fry lightly. Add 1/2 cup of the reserved bamboo shoot liquid and a pinch ground ginger. Bring to the boil and simmer. Add the pepper to the skillet when the onions are transparent, and stew briefly with the other vegetables. Season with the curry powder, sugar and soy sauce. Add the drained mushrooms to the skillet with the shrimp and peas. Warm the rice wine or sherry and pour over the dish before serving.

STIR-FRIED SHRIMP

1 onion, quartered
1/4 pound fresh bean sprouts,
  cleaned
1 large piece tender canned
  bamboo, drained
2 tablespoons oil
1/2 teaspoon salt
1 small piece root ginger,
  peeled and chopped

3/4 pound shrimp
1 stalk celery, chopped
2 tablespoons sake, Chinese
  rice wine or dry sherry
1/2 cup chicken stock
  (see page 7)
2 tablespoons cornstarch

Cut the onion quarters lengthways into strips. Put the bean sprouts in a pan and pour on boiling water. Rinse under the cold tap until completely cooled, then drain throughly. Cut the bamboo lengthwise into pieces 1 inch thick, then cut into strips.

Heat the oil in a wok or skillet. Add the salt and stir for 20 seconds over high heat. Add the ginger and the onion and continue stirring for 1 to 1 1/2 minutes. Add the bamboo and bean sprouts and fry for a further 30 to 40 seconds, turning the ingredients over thoroughly in the hot oil. Add the shrimps and celery and turn a few times in the oil. Pour in the sake (or rice wine, or sherry) round the edge of the pan and stir in. Add the stock.

To thicken the sauce, mix the cornstarch to a smooth paste with a little cold water in a cup. Blend a little of the hot liquid into the mixture, then return to the pan. Bring slowly to the boil and simmer gently for 2 to 3 minutes to allow the flour to cook through. Serve immediately.

MOW-TAN-MAZ

2 small pickled cucumbers,
  drained
2 cups cornstarch
2 eggs
½ cup water
½ cup oil
9 ounces canned chestnuts,
  drained and chopped

9 ounces canned shrimp,
  drained
salt, pepper
oil for frying
sprigs parsley
juice 1 lemon

Peel the cucumbers and cut into very small dice. Mix the cornstarch, eggs, water and oil to a smooth batter in a bowl. Stir in the chestnuts, shrimp and cucumber. Season to taste. Heat a little oil in a skillet. Ladle enough batter into the pan to make a small, thin crepe 4 inches across. Cook 3 minutes each side. Then remove from the pan, drain on absorbent paper and keep warm. Continue until all the batter is used, adding more frying oil to the pan when necessary. Stack the crepes on top of each other, in a warm oven to keep warm. Serve garnished with sprigs of parsley, and with lemon juice, served separately.

CRAB WITH SHERRY

3 ounces crabmeat
5 eggs
salt, pepper
2 teaspoons dry sherry
3 tablespoons oil
2 scallions *or* 1 small
  onion, finely chopped

2 ounces fresh mushrooms,
  sliced
1 tablespoon chopped chives
  or parsley

Drain the crabmeat, reserving the liquid, and remove any hard pieces of tendon. Set aside 2 pieces of crabmeat suitable for decoration. Beat the eggs in a bowl, stirring in ½ teaspoon salt, pepper to taste and the sherry. Heat 1½ tablespoons oil in a wok or skillet. Add the scallions and mushrooms and fry for 2 minutes, stirring all the time. Add the crabmeat and reserved liquid and cook over a high heat for 2 to 3 minutes, stirring continuously. Remove the pan from the heat and allow to cool until hand-hot.

Stir the contents of the pan into the egg mixture. Heat the remaining oil in another skillet, pour in the mixture, and fry over a fairly high heat until the underside begins to turn light brown. Turn the omelet over so that the other side sets quickly. Transfer the omelet to a hot serving plate, sprinkle with chives or parsley, and serve garnished with the reserved two pieces of uncooked crabmeat.

POULTRY

CHICKEN AND PINEAPPLE

2 pounds chicken, boned
1½ tablespoons cornstarch
5 tablespoons oil
4 tablespoons soy sauce
3 tablespoons dry sherry
salt, pepper
8 ounces canned pineapple
  chunks
1 clove garlic

Cut the chicken into pieces. Mix the cornstarch in a bowl with 3 tablespoons oil, the soy sauce and 1 tablespoon sherry. Season to taste. Add the chicken pieces to the marinade, cover and allow to stand for 30 minutes. Meanwhile drain the pineapple chunks and reserve the juice. Make the juice up to ½ cup with water if necessary. Crush the garlic with salt.

Heat the remaining oil in a skillet. Remove the chicken pieces from the marinade, drain and add to the pan. Reserve the marinade for making the sauce. Fry the chicken over medium heat for 5 minutes, stirring all the time. Add the pineapple chunks, cover the pan and continue frying over gentle heat for 12 minutes. Remove the chicken and pineapple from the pan, arrange on a warmed serving plate, cover and keep warm.

Add the garlic to the pan and fry for 5 minutes. Mix the pineapple juice with the remaining sherry and the marinade. Add to the pan and bring to the boil. Strain the sauce and pour it over the pieces of chicken and pineapple. Serve at once with saffron rice.

CHINESE CHICKEN WITH SHRIMP AND BAMBOO SHOOTS

1 pound chicken thighs or
  breasts, boned
salt, pepper
5 ounces canned bamboo
  shoots, drained
½ cup oil
5 ounces frozen shrimp
  thawed
¼ pound mushrooms,
  sliced
3 cups chicken
  stock (see page 7)
1½ tablespoons cornstarch
3 tablespoons soy sauce
1 teaspoon sugar
1 teaspoon sambal baatjak
  (see note below)
1 tablespoon spare rib sauce
  (see note below)
5 large shrimps, peeled

Cut the chicken pieces into strips and season with salt. Cut the bamboo shoots into strips. Heat the oil in a skillet, add the chicken and fry until golden brown (5 minutes). Add the bamboo shoots and fry for 15 minutes. Add the shrimp and mushrooms, and continue frying gently for 10 minutes, stirring from time to time.

Meanwhile make the sauce. Bring the stock to the boil in a pan. Mix the cornstarch to a smooth paste with a little cold water in a cup. Blend a little of the hot stock into the mixture, then return to the pan. Bring slowly to the boil, stirring constantly. Simmer for 2 to 3 minutes to allow the flour to cook through. Season with the soy sauce, sugar, salt and pepper. Add the sauce to the chicken and shrimp mixture. Cover the pan and leave to simmer, very gently, for 5 minutes. Adjust seasoning to taste with sambal baatjak and spare rib sauce.

Serve this dish with boiled, long-grain rice. Arrange the rice in a serving bowl, pour the chicken mixture into the center and garnish with large shrimp.

Note Sambal baatjak is an Indonesian relish and can be bought ready-prepared from oriental groceries. Spare rib sauce can also be bought ready-prepared.

Chinese chicken with Shrimp and Bamboo Shoots (opposite)

CHINESE FRIED CHICKEN

1 leek	ground ginger
2 pounds chicken	6 tablespoons flour
2 tablespoons soy sauce	1 egg
2 tablespoons Chinese rice wine or dry sherry	oil for deep frying

Cut the leek in half lengthways and cut into thin strips. Bring a large pan of lightly salted water to the boil. Add the chicken, leek, soy sauce, 1 tablespoon rice wine or sherry and a pinch ground ginger. Simmer for 1½ hours until the chicken is tender.

Remove the chicken from the pan and drain. Reserve 4 tablespoons of the chicken stock. Remove the bones from the chicken. Cut the meat into strips and allow to cool. Trickle the rest of the rice wine or sherry over the meat. While the chicken is cooling, mix the flour and egg to a smooth batter with the reserved chicken stock. Coat the chicken strips with the batter and deep fry in hot oil until golden brown. Drain on absorbent paper and serve at once.

DEMBARAN

3 pound chicken	2 tablespoons tamarind pulp, chopped
1 onion, chopped	
2 cloves garlic, crushed	salt
6 almonds, chopped	3 tablespoons oil
1½ teaspoons turmeric	⅓ coconut milk

Divide the chicken into 8 or 10 pieces. Pound together the onion, garlic, almonds, turmeric, and 1 teaspoon salt. Heat the oil in a casserole and fry the spices and seasonings for 3 minutes. Add the chicken pieces and brown over a moderate heat. Add the coconut milk and simmer for 45 minutes, or until the chicken is tender and the sauce has thickened. Stir from time to time to prevent sticking. Add a little extra water if necessary during cooking. Adjust seasoning and serve.

GANO

3 pounds chicken	4 eggs
¾ pound pork hock	1 teaspoon water
salt, pepper	oil for frying
½ pound shrimp, chopped	2 tablespoons shortening
2 cloves garlic, crushed	2 tablespoons soy sauce
2 tablespoons flour	3 leaves white cabbage, shredded
	1 celery leaf

Put the chicken and pork in a large saucepan. Season with salt and pour in enough cold water to cover. Bring to the boil, skim off the fat which rises to the surface and simmer, covered, for 2 hours, or until tender.

Pound the shrimp with half the garlic, and the salt, pepper and flour. Separately, beat the eggs with the water and season with salt. Melt a little oil in a skillet and make 2 omelets, using half the egg mixture for each. Only allow the undersides of the omelets to set. Put half the shrimp mixture into each omelet and roll them up. Finish cooking them in a steamer, over a pan of boiling water, until set. Then leave to cool for 30 minutes and cut them across into ½ inch slices.

Remove the chicken and pork from the stock. Strain the stock. Bone the chicken and pork and cut the meat into pieces. Melt the shortening in a heavy saucepan and fry the remaining garlic. Pour in the stock and bring to the boil. Simmer for 10 minutes. Add the meat, omelet slices, soy sauce, cabbage and celery leaf, and heat through. Serve at once in warmed bowls.

MO-KU-CHI-PIEN

1¾ pounds chicken
  drumsticks or breasts, boned
⅓ cup Chinese rice wine or
  dry sherry
1½ tablespoons flour
salt, pepper, ground ginger
⅓ cup oil

1 cup frozen peas, thawed
¼ pound fresh mushrooms
1 tablespoons soy sauce
¼ cup hot stock
1 teaspoon cornstarch

Cut the chicken meat into pieces and place in a bowl. Mix together ¼ cup of the rice wine or sherry and the flour in a cup. Season with salt and pepper. Pour this marinade over the chicken pieces, cover, and leave to stand for 10 minutes.

Heat 2 tablespoons of the oil in a skillet. Fry the peas and mushrooms for 2 minutes, stirring. Season with salt. Remove the vegetables from the pan and keep warm. Add the remaining oil to the pan and heat. Stir the chicken pieces and marinade into the pan and fry for 5 minutes, stirring all the time. Return the vegetables to the pan and mix with the chicken. Season to taste with salt, soy sauce, a small pinch ground ginger and the stock.

Mix the cornstarch to a smooth paste with the remaining rice wine or sherry and add to the pan, stirring. Let the contents of the pan come to the boil, adjust the seasoning if necessary, and serve.

SATE AYAM

2 pound chicken, skinned
  and boned
½ teaspoon salt
½ teaspoon belacan (shrimp
  paste)

2 cloves garlic, crushed
pepper
3 tablespoons soy sauce
1 tablespoon lemon juice
1 tablespoon oil

The chicken for this recipe should be young, fresh and tender. Cut the chicken meat into cubes suitable for threading on to skewers. In a basin, mash together the salt, belacan (shrimp paste), garlic and a pinch pepper. Add the soy sauce and lemon juice and stir well. Add the oil and chicken pieces. Stir thoroughly and leave to marinate for 30 minutes.

Remove the chicken pieces from the marinade, drain and thread them on to small kabob skewers. Grill over a barbeque if possible, although an ordinary gas or electric broiler will still produce good results. Baste with the marinade from time to time, and grill the kebabs until they are brown and tender. Serve immediately.

INDONESIAN CHICKEN KABOBS

4 chicken breasts (10 ounces each), skinned and boned	salt, pepper
chopped walnut meats	1 clove garlic
1 cup lime juice or lemon juice	1 onion, chopped
1 cup hot chicken stock (see page 7)	2 tablespoons oil
	½ cup heavy cream
	sprigs parsley

Cut the chicken into pieces suitable for threading on skewers. Mix the walnuts, lime or lemon juice, stock, salt and pepper in a bowl. Crush the garlic with salt and add to the marinade with the onion. Put one third of the marinade aside and add the chicken pieces to the remainder. Cover and allow to stand for 3 hours.

Drain the chicken and pat dry on absorbent paper. Thread the chicken pieces on to skewers and brush them with the oil. Cover the rack of the broiler with aluminium foil, place the skewers on it and grill for 20 minutes, turning once. Drain the reserved marinade and mix with the cream to make a sauce. Heat gently in a pan without boiling. Serve the skewers on a warmed plate and garnish with the sprigs parsley. Hand the sauce separately.

ORIENTAL SPICED CHICKEN

2 chickens (1¾ pounds each)	4 tablespoons light cream
2 teaspoons curry powder	2 tablespoons lemon juice
2 teaspoons mild paprika	1 teaspoon ground coriander
1 teaspoon black pepper	1 teaspoon ground cardamum
salt	oil for deep frying
2 tablespoons oil	

Cut each chicken into 4 pieces. Mix together the curry powder, paprika, pepper and a pinch salt on a plate. Toss the chicken pieces in this mixture and place them in a shallow bowl. Stir the oil, cream and lemon juice together in a jug, and pour over the chicken pieces. Sprinkle with the coriander and cardamum. Allow to stand for 30 minutes, turning from time to time. Remove the chicken pieces from the marinade and pat dry with absorbent paper.

Heat the oil to a temperature of 350°F. Deep fry the chicken portions, in 2 batches of 4, for 15 minutes each. Keep the first batch hot while you fry the second. Arrange in a warmed bowl and serve.

Indonesian Chicken Kabobs (opposite)

SINGGANG AYAM

2 pound chicken	½ teaspoon turmeric
1 small onion, chopped	½ teaspoon galingale
2 cloves garlic, crushed	(optional)
½ teaspoon chilli paste	1 teaspoon salt
small slice root ginger,	1 piece lemon grass (optional)
chopped	2 cups coconut milk
½ teaspoon pepper	

The chicken for this recipe should be young, fresh and tender. Cut the chicken open down the breast. Open the two halves outwards and press flat by breaking the breast bones where they are attached to the back. Push a wooden skewer through the legs and the back so that the bird is held flat, and skewer the wings into position in the same way. Pound and mix together all the ingredients except the lemon grass and coconut milk. Rub the mixture into the chicken meat and leave for 1½ hours to absorb the flavors.

Bring the coconut milk to the boil in a large saucepan. Add the lemon grass and chicken. Simmer over moderate heat, with the pan uncovered, until the chicken is almost done (45 minutes to 1 hour). Then remove the chicken from the pan and grill it over the barbeque until golden brown. Tickle some of the cooking liquid over it from time to time. Remove the skewers and serve.

CHICKEN IN SOY SAUCE

3 pounds chicken, skinned	1 egg white
and boned	1 leek
1 tablespoon cornstarch	½ cup oil
2 tablespoons Chinese rice	1 pound canned bean sprouts,
wine or dry sherry	drained
3 tablespoons soy sauce	pepper, ground ginger

Cut the chicken into thin pieces about 1¼ inches in size. Mix the cornstarch in a bowl with the rice wine or sherry and 1 tablespoon soy sauce. Beat the egg white lightly with a fork and stir into the marinade. Add the chicken pieces and allow to stand for 30 minutes.

Meanwhile cut the leek in half lengthways and then into thin strips ¾ inch long. Heat half of the oil in a large, shallow skillet. Fry the leek for 3 minutes, stirring. Add the bean sprouts and fry for another 2 minutes. Season with pepper, the remaining soy sauce and a small pinch ground ginger. Heat the remaining oil in another skillet. Remove the chicken pieces from the marinade, drain and fry in the oil for 5 minutes until golden brown on all sides. Then transfer to the vegetable skillet and fry for another 3 minutes, stirring all the time. Arrange on a warmed plate and serve at once.

BEBEK-BUMBU BALI

4 pounds duck
2 teaspoons salt
2 onions chopped
3 cloves garlic, crushed
3 chilli peppers, chopped *or*
  1½ teaspoons chilli sauce
1 teaspoon turmeric
2 teaspoons galingale
  (optional)

belacan (shrimp paste)
3 tablespoons oil
3 tablespoons soy sauce
2 pieces lemon grass
  (optional)
1 bay leaf
2 cups boiling water

Clean the duck and cut it into 4 pieces. Pound and mix together the salt, onions, garlic, chilli pepper or sauce, turmeric, galingale and a little belacan (prawn paste). Heat the oil in a large, heavy pan and fry the spices in it for 3 minutes. Add the duck pieces and soy sauce and continue frying until the duck pieces are brown. Add the lemon grass, bay leaf and water. Cover the pan, bring to the boil, and simmer for 40 minutes, or until the duck is tender. Stir from time to time to prevent sticking. If necessary add more hot water. When the duck is cooked, boil away as much of the liquid as possible. Transfer to a warmed plate and serve with boiled, long-grain rice.

CHINESE DUCK

2 cups + 5 tablespoons dry
  sherry
2 tablespoons honey
2 tablespoons soy sauce
2 small pieces preserved stem
  ginger, chopped
1 teaspoon mustard powder
1 teaspoon sesame seeds
3 pounds duck, ready to roast
salt
3 tablespoons margarine

rind ½ orange
juice 6 oranges
2 tablespoons sugar
1½ tablespoons cornstarch
7 ounces canned mandarin
  oranges, drained
1 banana, sliced
1 orange, sliced
2 cherries
sprigs parsley

Mix 2 cups of the sherry with the honey and soy sauce. Stir in half the ginger, the mustard powder and sesame seeds. Marinate the duck in this mixture for 3 hours, covered, turning the duck from time to time. Take the duck out of the marinade, drain well and season with salt inside. Melt the margarine in a roasting pan and brown the duck on all sides. Then place the pan in the oven and roast for 1 hour 10 minutes at 400°F, basting with the marinade every so often.

Cut the orange rind into very thin strips. Chop the remaining ginger very finely. Mix together the orange rind and juice, ginger, sugar and 2½ tablespoons sherry in a pan. Heat gently. Mix the cornstarch to a smooth paste in a cup with the remaining sherry. Blend a little of the hot liquid into the mixture, then return to the pan. Bring slowly to the boil, stirring constantly. Simmer for 2 to 3 minutes to allow the flour to cook through. Then add half of the mandarin oranges and banana slices to the sauce and heat through gently.

Place the cooked duck on a warmed serving plate. Arrange the remaining mandarin oranges, and the slices of orange topped with the remaining banana slices, around the duck. Garnish with the cherries and sprigs parsley. Hand the sauce separately.

PEKING DUCK

3 pounds duck
⅓ cup water

4–5 tablespoons honey

Peking duck is one of the most famous of all Chinese dishes; its special feature is the crisp, tasty skin which is served separately.

Ask the poulterer for a good duck, as fresh as possible. The feathers should be on, the skin as intact as possible, and the bird should still have its neck, with skin. Pluck the bird. Plunge in boiling water long enough to blanch the skin. Dry thoroughly, inside and out. Skewer or stitch up the vent firmly. Tie a piece of string under the wings and round the neck, and hang in a cool, well-ventilated place, by an open window for example, for a couple of hours until the skin is completely dry.

Bring the water to the boil and stir in the honey until fully dissolved. Leave to cool until tepid, then spread the honey mixture over the duck in several applications, pausing after each one, until the skin is impregnated with the honey. Hang the bird up again until the skin has completely dried.

Place the duck on a rack in a roasting pan. Roast until the duck is brown, 1 to 1½ hours at 375°F. Check that the skin browns evenly; any patches that look like turning too dark should be covered with aluminum foil. The duck is then removed from the oven and the skin is removed and carved into long, thin strips.

The correct way to eat Peking duck is with pancakes, hoisin or plum sauce and scallion tassels (see page 76). A slice of skin and a scallion tassel are placed on a sauce-covered pancake, which is then rolled up and eaten with the fingers.

Notes Before being sewn up and hung to dry, the duck can be smeared inside with a paste made up of ½ teaspoon salt, ½ teaspoon hoisin, 1 teaspoon soy sauce, ½ teaspoon five-spice powder, and 1 tablespoon rice wine or sherry.

Sometimes a slit is made in the skin where the neck joins the body. a straw is inserted and air is blown under the skin so that it comes away from the flesh and balloons out. The neck is then tied with string just below the slit. This treatment makes the skin even crisper and tastier.

Traditional Peking duck is a dish which, even in China, is almost exclusively prepared by experts in restaurants where it is a speciality. Because of the specially-bred ducks, the elaborate and time-consuming preparation and special oven in which the duck should be roasted, the same sort of result should not be expected when prepared at home.

Meat

Cantonese Pork

2 pounds lean pork, without
  skin or bones
1 tablespoon soy sauce
2 tablespoons chicken stock
  (see page 7)
1 tablespoon honey

1 tablespoon sugar
1 teaspoon dayong (see note
  below)
salt
2 tablespoons olive oil

Pat the pork dry with absorbent paper. Mix the soy sauce, stock, honey, sugar and dayong in a bowl. Season with salt. Spread this mixture over the pork and rub well in. Put the pork in a bowl, cover and leave to stand for 1 hour. Remove and drain, reserving the marinade. Rub the oil into the pork, put in a casserole, and paint with the reserved marinade. Cover and place on the middle shelf of the oven. Bake for 1 hour 20 minutes at 400°F. Remove from the oven and serve in the casserole with a bamboo shoot salad, boiled, long-grain rice and mushrooms.

Note Dayong is obtainable ready-prepared from oriental groceries.

Cantonese Pork

CHINESE FAT BACK

2 pounds lean fat back, with
  the rind on
garlic salt, ground star anise,
  ground ginger
1 tablespoon soy sauce
2 tablespoons coconut oil
1 cup hot water
1 sweet red pepper, sliced
2 cloves star anise

SAUCE
½ pound sweet red peppers,
  seeded and chopped
1 ounce canned apricots,
  drained
1 clove garlic
salt
grated rind ½ lemon
1 tablespoon chilli sauce
2 tablespoons soy sauce

Wash and scrub the pork rind and pat dry with absorbent paper. Make cuts across it to form a diamond pattern. Mix together a pinch each garlic salt, ground star anise and ground ginger in a bowl with the soy sauce and coconut oil. Rub this mixture well into the meat. Lay the meat on a rack in a roasting pan, and place on the middle shelf of the oven. Pour the water into the roasting pan and roast for 1 hour 40 minutes at 400°F. Baste the roast from time to time with the liquid from the pan. While the meat is roasting, make the sauce.

Bring a pan of lightly salted water to the boil. Add the peppers and simmer for 20 minutes. Drain and cool slightly. Blend the peppers with the apricots in a blender, or strain through a sieve to make a purée. Crush the garlic clove with salt and mix into the pepper and apricot purée. Add the lemon rind, chilli sauce and soy sauce, and mix.

Take the meat out of the oven and arrange on a warmed plate. Garnish with the red pepper and cloves star anise. Serve the sauce separately with a bowl of boiled, long-grain rice.

CHINESE ROAST FAT BACK

2 pounds lean fat back, with
  the rind on
salt
½ tablespoon brown sugar

2 tablespoons soy sauce
1 teaspoon chopped root
  ginger
hoisin sauce (optional)

Prick holes in the pork rind and rub well with salt. Mix together the sugar, soy sauce, ginger and hoisin sauce if desired. Rub this mixture into the other side of the pork. Place the pork on a flat tray or broiler pan with the rind uppermost, and grill for 20 minutes, until the rind is crisp all over. Transfer to the oven and roast for 1 hour at 350°F. Remove from the oven and allow to cool to room temperature. Cut the meat into small chunks and serve with stir-fried Chinese cabbage (see page 74).

Watercress and scallions are also good accompaniments to this dish.

CHINESE ROAST FAT BACK WITH BEAN CURD

½ the ingredients for Chinese roast fat back (see page 38)
1 pad bean curd
2-3 tablespoons soy sauce
½ cup chicken stock (see page 7)
½ teaspoon salt
½ teaspoon sugar
1 tablespoon cornstarch
2 tablespoons water
1½ tablespoons oil
sprigs parsley

Prepare and cook the roast fat back as described on page 38, but using half the ingredients and a shorter roasting time (about 45 minutes). Remove from the oven when cooked and allow to cool.

While the pork is cooking cut the bean curd into chunks 1½ × ¾ × ¾ inch. When the pork has cooled cut it into similar-sized chunks. Put the soy sauce, stock, salt and sugar in a saucepan. Heat the mixture until the salt and sugar dissolve. Mix the cornstarch to a smooth paste in a cup with the water.

Heat the oil in a wok or skillet. Add the bean curd and fry, stirring, until just colored on all sides. Pour on the soy sauce mixture and simmer over low heat for 7 minutes. Add the cornstarch paste and stir, over high heat, until the sauce is thick and shiny. Add the pork to the pan and heat through. Sprinkle with parsley and serve, with boiled, long-grain rice.

BABI CIN

1¾ pounds fat pork
2 cloves garlic, crushed
small piece root ginger, chopped or 1 teaspoon ground ginger
½ teaspoon ground coriander
1 tablespoon soy-bean paste
2 tablespoons soy sauce
salt, pepper
¼ cup shortening
1-2 cups hot stock
½ pound small potatoes
6 shallots, halved
2 scallions, finely chopped
½ stalk celery, finely chopped

Cut the pork (boned pork shoulder for example) into squares. Pound and mix together the garlic, ginger, coriander and soy-bean paste. Stir in the soy sauce and season with salt and pepper. Add the meat and mix thoroughly.

Heat 2 tablespoons shortening in a saucepan, add the meat and brown on all sides. Add 1 cup stock, bring to the boil, reduce the heat and simmer gently until all the fat has been drawn out.

Meanwhile heat the remaining shortening in another pan. Add the potatoes and fry gently until almost done (test with a fork). Remove and keep warm. Add the shallots to the pan in which the potatoes were cooked, and fry for a few minutes. Skim off the fat which will have risen to the top of the meat pan. Then add the potatoes and shallots to the meat, pouring on more stock if necessary. Add the scallions and celery and simmer for a further 5 minutes before serving.

BABI KECAP

1¾ pounds pork, cubed
salt, pepper
1 small onion, chopped
2 cloves garlic, crushed
small piece root ginger,
  chopped

1 red chilli pepper, chopped
  or ½ teaspoon chilli sauce
1 teaspoon lemon juice
2 tablespoons oil
5 tablespoons soy sauce
boiling water

Pork with some fat attached is best for this recipe. Season the pork cubes. Mix together the onion, garlic, ginger, chilli and lemon juice. Add the pork and leave to marinate for 10 minutes.

Heat the oil in a saucepan and lightly fry the meat and seasonings. Add the soy sauce, stir, and pour over just enough boiling water to cover the meat. Bring to the boil, reduce the heat and simmer, adding more hot water if necessary, until the meat is tender and the fat has been drawn out. The simmering time will depend on the cut of meat. When cooked, skim off the fat which will have risen to the surface of the pan, adjust the seasoning and serve immediately.

CHINESE LIVER

1 pound pig's liver
flour for coating
1 red pepper, seeded
1 green pepper, seeded
½ pound cabbage
5 tablespoons oil
salt, pepper
3 tablespoons soy sauce
2 tablespoons Chinese rice
  wine or dry sherry

½ pound onions, sliced
1 cup stock
5 ounces canned bean sprouts,
  drained or 5 ounces fresh
  bean sprouts, cleaned
5 ounces canned bamboo
  shoots, drained and chopped

Pat the liver dry with absorbent paper and cut it into narrow strips. Toss in the flour. Cut the peppers and cabbage into strips. Heat the oil in a skillet, add the liver and brown on all sides. Remove from the pan, drain, season to taste and keep warm. Add the soy sauce and rice wine or sherry to the pan. Add the onions and simmer for 5 minutes. Add the stock, peppers and cabbage and simmer for about 10 minutes, until just tender. Return the liver to the pan. Add the bean sprouts and bamboo shoots. Reheat and serve with boiled, long-grain rice and extra soy sauce sprinkled on top if desired.

Chinese Liver

40

SZECHUAN PORK

1¾ pounds lean leg of pork
½ cup oil
¼ pound fresh mushrooms, sliced
½ pound green peppers, seeded and chopped
½ pound tomatoes, sliced
salt, ground ginger
½ pound onions, finely chopped
1 clove garlic, crushed
2 tablespoons dry sherry
1 cup hot stock
1 tablespoon soy sauce
2 tablespoons cornstarch

Cut the pork into thin strips 2 inches long. Heat 4 tablespoons oil in a skillet. Add the mushrooms, peppers and tomatoes and fry gently for 5 minutes. Remove from the pan, drain and keep warm. Heat the remaining oil in another pan. Add the meat. Sprinkle with salt and a pinch ground ginger and fry for 10 minutes, stirring. Then add the onions and garlic and fry for another 5 minutes. Pour in the sherry and heat through briefly. Then add the stock and soy sauce. Finally, add the reserved mushroom, pepper and tomato mixture. Cover the pan and stew gently over medium heat for 25 minutes.

Mix the cornstarch to a smooth paste in a cup with a little cold water. Blend a little of the hot liquid into the mixture, then return to the pan. Bring slowly to the boil, stirring constantly. Simmer for 2 to 3 minutes to allow the flour to cook through. Transfer the contents of the pan to a warmed bowl and serve.

DAGING MASAK TOMAT

1 pound pork
5 ripe tomatoes, skinned, seeded and chopped
4 red onions, chopped
small piece root ginger, chopped or 2 teaspoons ground ginger
2–3 red chilli peppers, chopped or 2 teaspoons chilli sauce
1 piece lemon grass (optional)
½ teaspoon sugar
1 teaspoon salt
1 cup water
1 scallion, chopped or 2 teaspoons chopped chives

Cut the pork, which should be edged with fat, into chunks. Thoroughly mix together all the remaining ingredients, except for the water and scallion or chives. Put the mixed ingredients into a saucepan, add the water and bring to the boil. Reduce the heat and simmer gently for 45 minutes to 1 hour, until the meat is cooked and the sauce has thickened, adding a little extra water if necessary. Just before serving, stir in the scallion or chives, allowing 1½ to 2 minutes for the scallion to heat through, and 30 seconds for the chives. Serve immediately.

TERIYAKI STEAK

4 sirloin steaks (½ pound each)
1 clove garlic
salt, pepper
2 tablespoons candied ginger, finely chopped
1½ tablespoons brown sugar
½ cup Chinese rice wine or dry sherry
½ cup soy sauce
½ cup white wine
juice ½ lemon
4 tomatoes
canned bean sprouts, drained
1 tablespoon tomato catsup

Teriyaki is a Japanese seasoning made on a base of soy sauce.

Pat the steaks dry with absorbent paper. Make a marinade as follows: crush the garlic with salt. Mix the garlic and ginger in a shallow bowl with the sugar, rice wine or sherry, soy sauce, white wine and lemon juice. Season with salt and pepper. Put the steaks in the marinade and turn several times. Cover and leave to stand for 12 hours. Turn from time to time during the marinating period.

Cut out any hard parts from the tomato stems. Cut a lid off the tomatoes and scoop out the seeds. Season the insides with salt and pepper. Put the bean sprouts in a pan with the tomato catsup and heat, stirring, for 5 minutes. Stuff the tomatoes with this mixture.

Drain the steaks well. Put them on a broiler rack, with the broiler pan underneath, and grill 4 minutes each side. Arrange the steaks on warmed plates, garnish with the tomatoes, and serve at once with boiled, long-grain rice.

PEKING BEEF

1 pound sirloin steak
5 tablespoons soy sauce
1 tablespoon Chinese rice wine or dry sherry
1 cup oil
flour for coating
2 cloves garlic
salt, ground ginger, ground aniseed
2 leeks, finely sliced
1 tablespoon ginger syrup (from jar preserved stem ginger)
½ cup stock
1 teaspoon cornstarch

Pat the meat dry with absorbent paper. Cut into very thin slices diagonally, across the grain of the meat. Mix 3 tablespoons of the soy sauce with the rice wine or sherry in a deep bowl. Add the meat, cover, and leave to marinate for 1 hour.

Heat the oil in a skillet. Take the meat out of the marinade, drain well and dust with flour. Add to the oil and fry for 3 minutes. Remove the meat, drain and set aside. Take 4 tablespoons of the frying oil and put in another pan. Crush the garlic cloves with salt. Heat the 4 tablespoons oil, add the garlic and leeks, and fry for 5 minutes, stirring. Add the meat. Season with the ginger syrup, a pinch ground ginger, the remaining soy sauce and a small pinch ground aniseed. Pour the stock into the pan. Remove from the heat and allow to stand, covered for 1 hour to draw out the flavors.

Return the pan to the stove and heat gently. Mix the cornstarch to a smooth paste in a cup with a little cold water. Blend a little of the hot liquid into the mixture, then return to the pan. Bring slowly to the boil, stirring constantly. Simmer for 2 to 3 minutes. Adjust the seasoning, transfer to a warmed bowl and serve.

Note As an alternative to ginger syrup use honey instead, but increase the amount of ground ginger to 1 teaspoon.

MONGOLIAN FONDUE

2 pounds tender beef

CHICKEN BROTH
1½ quarts chicken stock (see page 7)
2 carrots, sliced
1 leek, sliced
¼ celeriac root, chopped
1 tablespoon chopped parsley

TARTARE SAUCE
½ cup mayonnaise
2 tablespoons small capers
2 tablespoons chopped chives
2 gherkins, finely chopped
2 teaspoons lemon juice

2 teaspoons lemon juice
2 tablespoons canned evaporated milk
salt, pepper
sugar

CATSUP SAUCE
½ cup mayonnaise
2 tablespoons tomato catsup
1 teaspoon Worcestershire sauce
sambal (see note below)
curry sauce
sugar
salt

Pat the meat dry with absorbent paper. Cut into thin slices, about the thickness of sliced salami. Bring the chicken stock to the boil on the stove, in the fondue pot. Add the carrots, leek, celeriac and parsley, and simmer for 20 minutes.

To make the tartare sauce, mix the mayonnaise with the capers, chives, gherkins and lemon juice. Stir in the evaporated milk until the sauce is creamy. Season to taste with salt, pepper and a pinch sugar.

To make the catsup sauce, mix together the mayonnaise, tomato catsup and Worcestershire sauce. Stir in a small amount of sambal and a dash of curry sauce. Season to taste with a pinch each sugar and salt.

Arrange the meat, tartare sauce and catsup sauce in separate bowls on the table. Place the chicken broth, simmering gently in the fondue pot, over its flame on the table. As it evaporates, top it up with boiling water. Each guest wraps a slice of meat round his fondue fork, dips it into the simmering broth, and leaves it there for at least 1 minute to cook the beef through. The meat is then dipped into the sauces and eaten. Serve with boiled, long-grain rice.

Note Sambal is an Indonesian relish, available ready-prepared, in several different varieties, from oriental groceries.

CHINESE FONDUE

2 pounds sirloin steak (or use half each pork and veal tenderloin)
1 quart good beef stock

2 tablespoons white wine or whisky
3 teaspoons soy sauce

Remove all fat and white skin from the meat. Cut into thin slices, about the thickness of sliced salami, and arrange on plates in individual portions. Heat the stock on the stove in the fondue pot. Flavor it with the white wine or whisky, and soy sauce. Put the fondue pot over its flame in the center of the table. Every guest spears a slice of meat on his fondue fork, dips it into the boiling stock and lets it cook for 1 minute. The meat is then dipped into various spicy accompaniments and sauces (see **Note**) before being eaten. When all the meat has been eaten, the stock in which it was cooked is poured into small cups and drunk as a soup.

Good accompaniments to a Chinese fondue are well-flavored sauces such as curry-flavored mayonnaise, rémoulade sauce, apple and horseradish cream, fruits in mustard pickle, small pickled onions and sweet-and-sour gherkins. They can be bought ready-prepared or made at home.

Mongolian Fondue

DAGING SEMOR

1-1¼ pounds beef with a little fat, cubed	¼–½ teaspoon ground nutmeg
1 onion, chopped	galingale (optional)
1 clove garlic, crushed	1 tablespoon soy sauce
small piece root ginger, chopped or 1 teaspoon ground ginger	1 chilli pepper, chopped or 1 teaspoon chilli sauce
½ teaspoon salt	1 bay leaf
½ teaspoon pepper	1 piece lemon grass
	1 tablespoon oil

Mix together the meat, onion, garlic, ginger, salt, pepper, nutmeg, a pinch galingale, soy sauce and chilli, and put in a saucepan. Add just enough water to cover the meat. Add the bay leaf, lemon grass and oil, and bring to the boil. Reduce the heat, partly cover the pan, and simmer gently until the meat is tender and the water almost evaporated. The simmering time will depend on the cut of the meat. If necessary add a little more hot water from time to time during cooking. Serve immediately.

CHINESE STEAK WITH GREEN PEPPERS

1 pound sirloin steak	salt, ground ginger
1½ tablespoons cornstarch	oil for frying
2 tablespoons dry sherry	2 green peppers, seeded and chopped
3 tablespoons soy sauce	
1 tablespoon sugar	

Cut the steak into thin slices. Trim off any fat and cut each slice into four. Mix the cornstarch, sherry, soy sauce, sugar and a pinch ground ginger in a bowl. Turn the pieces of meat in this marinade, cover, and leave to stand, preferably in the refrigerator, for 3 hours to absorb the flavors, turning from time to time.

Heat the oil to a very high temperature in a large skillet. Remove the meat from the marinade, pat it dry with absorbent paper, and fry for 5 minutes, shaking the pan to prevent the meat sticking. Remove from the pan, drain and transfer to a warmed serving bowl. Keep warm. Add the peppers to the pan and fry for 5 minutes. Season with salt. Remove from the pan, drain and use to garnish the meat. Serve at once.

DENDENG RAGI

1 pound lean beef
1½ cups fresh coconut, grated
  or 1½ cups shredded
  coconut
1 tablespoon coriander seeds,
  crushed
1 teaspoon ground cumin
2 cloves garlic, crushed
1 small onion, chopped
salt, pepper
1 chilli pepper, chopped or ½
  teaspoon hot soy sauce
4 tablespoons oil
2 tablespoons hot water
2 tablespoons tamarind juice

Cut the beef across the grain into thin slices approximately 2¼ × 1¼ inches. If using shredded coconut soak it with 1 tablespoon water. Pound and mix together the coriander, cumin, garlic, onion, pepper and chilli pepper or hot soy sauce. Heat 2 tablespoons of the oil in a pan, add the spices and fry. Add the meat slices and continue frying. Add the coconut and hot water, and simmer over a low heat until the moisture has been absorbed. Then add the tamarind juice and salt, and simmer, stirring occasionally, until all the moisture has been absorbed or evaporated, and the mixture is as dry as possible.

Heat the remaining oil separately. Pour this into the pan and fry the meat and coconut over a low heat until crisp and brown, turning from time to time to prevent the mixture sticking. Remove the meat from the pan and drain thoroughly on absorbent paper. Mix the fried coconut and meat together and serve with boiled, long-grain rice.

PEKING BREAKFAST

⅓ ounce dried Chinese
  mushrooms
1 pound sirloin steak
1 tablespoon soy sauce
½ cup water
1 teaspoon lemon juice
1 tablespoon dry sherry
4 tablespoons oil
1 leek, sliced
salt
sugar
4 ounce jar mussels, drained
1 teaspoon chilli sauce

Soak the mushrooms in warm water for 15 to 30 minutes, until swollen. Meanwhile, cut the meat first into thin slices, and then into narrow strips. Mix together the soy sauce, water, lemon juice and sherry in a cup. Drain the mushrooms thoroughly.

Heat the oil in a large skillet until it begins to smoke. Add the meat and fry, turning frequently, for 5 minutes. Add the leek and mushrooms, and continue frying, stirring all the time, for 4 minutes. Season with a pinch each salt and sugar. Add the mussels and pour the soy sauce and sherry mixture into the pan. Stir in the chilli sauce. Simmer over a very low heat for 5 minutes, then serve.

CANTONESE STEAK

1¼ pounds sirloin steak, in
  one piece
3 tablespoons oil
1 piece preserved stem ginger,
  finely chopped
½ clove garlic, finely chopped
grated rind ½ orange

MARINADE
2 tablespoons cornstarch
baking powder
1 teaspoon ginger syrup (from
  jar preserved stem ginger)
1 teaspoon fresh orange juice
1 tablespoon Chinese rice
  wine or dry sherry
1 tablespoon soy sauce

½ cup water
salt
sugar
3 tablespoons coconut or
  sesame seed oil

SAUCE
2 tablespoons tomato catsup
1 tablespoon Chinese rice
  wine or dry sherry
2 tablespoons water
salt
sugar
Worcestershire sauce
4 drops Tabasco sauce
1 tablespoon coconut oil

Trim off any fat or skin from the steak, pat dry with absorbent paper and carve into 12 thin slices. Beat flat with the ball of the hand. To make the marinade, mix the cornstarch and a small pinch baking powder in a bowl. Add the ginger syrup, orange juice, rice wine or sherry, soy sauce and water. Stir all together and season with salt and sugar. Finally stir in the oil. Rub this marinade into the meat and leave, covered, for 1 hour.

Heat the 3 tablespoons oil in a large skillet. Add the ginger, garlic and orange rind to the hot oil, then add the meat at once. Fry on each side for 2 minutes. Remove from the pan and keep hot on a warmed plate.

To make the sauce: add the tomato catsup, rice wine or sherry, and water to the hot oil in the pan and mix. Season to taste with salt, sugar, Worcestershire sauce and the Tabasco sauce. Put the steaks back in the sauce, stir in the last tablespoon of oil, and heat through. Serve immediately in a warmed bowl.

TOKYO STEAK

4 sirloin steaks (¼ pound
  each)
1 tablespoon green
  peppercorns
2 tablespoons Chinese rice
  wine or dry sherry
salt, ground ginger

butter for frying
¾ pound canned mandarin
  oranges, drained
1½ tablespoons butter, cut
  into flakes

Pat the steaks dry with absorbent paper. Mix the peppercorns and rice wine or sherry in a bowl. Season with salt and ground ginger. Rub this mixture well into the steaks. Heat the butter in a skillet. Add the steaks and fry for 2 minutes each side. Remove the steaks from the pan and arrange them on a broiler rack, with the broiler pan underneath to catch the drips. Place the mandarin oranges on top of the steaks and scatter on the flakes of butter. Grill for 3 minutes. Arrange the steaks on a warmed serving plate and serve with fried bean sprouts, boiled, long-grain rice and sake.

Tokyo Steak

SATE PADANG

1 teaspoon salt
1 pound beef, cubed
1 onion, chopped
2 cloves garlic, crushed
1 teaspoon chilli sauce
small piece root ginger, chopped
½ teaspoon galingale (optional)

½ teaspoon pepper
1 teaspoon turmeric
½ teaspoon ground coriander
1 teaspoon ground cumin
2 pieces lemon grass (optional)
2 tablespoons rice powder or 2 tablespoons cornstarch

Rub the salt into the meat cubes. Pound and mix together the onion, garlic, chilli sauce, ginger, galingale, pepper, turmeric, coriander and cumin. Put three quarters of this spicy marinade into a saucepan. Add the meat and stir. Allow to stand for 15 minutes so that the meat absorbs all the flavors. Then add just enough water to cover the meat. Bring to the boil, reduce the heat, add the lemon grass and simmer, with the pan partly covered, until the meat is nearly cooked but still firm.

Remove the meat from the pan and allow to drain. Add the remaining marinade to the pan and continue to simmer. Carefully thread the pieces of meat on to small kabob skewers and finish cooking by grilling, preferably on a barbeque, until well browned. Baste occasionally with the marinade sauce during the cooking.

Mix the rice powder or cornstarch to a smooth paste in a cup with a little cold water. Blend a little of the hot marinade into the mixture, then return to the pan. Bring slowly to the boil, stirring constantly. Simmer for 2 to 3 minutes to allow the flour to cook through. Arrange the meat on warmed plates, pour the sauce over and serve as part of a Malaysian or Indonesian-style dinner.

Note Great care should be taken not to let the meat get too tender at the braising stage, as it still has to be grilled.

SATE BALI

4 shallots, chopped
3 cloves garlic, crushed
1 piece lemon grass (optional)
small piece root ginger, chopped or ½ teaspoon ground ginger
1 teaspoon ground coriander
1 teaspoon belacan (shrimp paste) or 1 tablespoon shrimps
1 teaspoon tamarind pulp or 1 date, finely chopped
½ chilli pepper, finely chopped or ½ teaspoon chilli sauce

½ teaspoon turmeric or ½ teaspoon curry powder
2 teaspoons salt
juice ½ lemon
½ pound pork tenderloin, cubed
½ pound lamb from leg or shoulder, cubed
2 tablespoons oil
2 tablespoons coconut milk
butter
1 tablespoon soy sauce

Pound and mix together the shallots, garlic, lemon grass, ginger, coriander, belacan, tamarind, chilli, turmeric and salt. Stir in the lemon juice. Add the meat, stir well, and leave to marinate for at least 1 hour. Remove the meat from the marinade and drain, reserving the marinade. Thread the meat on to small skewers (about 5 pieces to a skewer) and brush with oil. Barbecue or grill on a rack under the broiler, with the broiler pan underneath to catch the drips, turning from time to time. Baste with the oil during cooking.

The left-over marinade can be used for an accompanying sauce, thinned with the coconut milk and, if necessary, a knob of butter and the soy sauce. This mixture is heated up and handed separately in a small bowl.

ORIENTAL FONDUE

Serves 6

½ pound pork tenderloin	2 tablespoons oil
½ pound sirloin steak	2 tablespoons Chinese rice
½ pound calves' liver	wine or dry sherry
½ pound fillets of sole	3 eggs
½ pound chicken breast,	½ pound spinach, washed and
skinned and boned	picked over
1 pound celery	2 quarts chicken stock (see
¼ pound transparent noodles	page 7)
2 tablespoons soy sauce	

Pat the pork, beef, liver, fish and chicken dry with absorbent paper. Place in the freezing compartment of the refrigerator for 30 minutes; this will enable you to cut them very thin with a sharp knife. Cut them into strips 3 inches long and ¾ inch wide. Cut the celery into similar-sized strips, blanch in boiling water for 4 minutes, drain and pat dry. Soak the noodles for 30 minutes in warm water. Drain and cut into pieces 4 inches long.

Make a sauce as follows: beat together the soy sauce, oil, rice wine or sherry and eggs. Put 1 tablespoon into a small bowl for each person. Arrange the meat, fish, chicken, noodles, celery and spinach in small bowls and place on the table. Heat the chicken stock to boiling point, pour into a fondue pot or casserole container, and stand over a burner in the center of the table.

Lay the table with a fondue fork and an empty bowl for each person. Each guest puts some meat in his bowl, spikes it on his fork and cooks it for 1 minute in the chicken stock. When it is done he dips it into his sauce and eats it. The meat and fish are eaten first, which gives the chicken stock added flavor. Then the noodles and vegetables are boiled for 1 minute in the remaining stock. Each guest has a portion and can dip his noodles and vegetables in any sauce he has left.

CHINESE HOTPOT

Serves 6

6 eggs	2 leeks, sliced
⅓ cup soy sauce	2 cups frozen shrimp,
4 chicken breasts, skinned	thawed
and boned	½ pound fresh mushrooms,
4 chicken livers	sliced
½ pound sirloin steak	½ pound fresh bean sprouts,
½ pound pork tenderloin	cleaned
10 ounces canned bamboo	1½ quarts chicken
shoots, drained	stock (see page 7)

Beat together the eggs and soy sauce; divide this mixture between six bowls, placing one at each place setting. Cut the chicken breasts and livers into thin strips. Cut the sirloin steak and pork tenderloin into thin slices the thickness of sliced salami. Cut the bamboo shoots into thin strips. Blanch the leeks in hot water and drain. Put these ingredients, and the shrimp, mushrooms and bean sprouts, into bowls and arrange on the table. Heat the chicken stock on the stove in a fondue pot. When it has come to the boil place the dish over its burner in the center of the table.

Each guest helps himself to a selection of raw ingredients from the bowls on the table. Using a fondue fork, he then spikes one or more items, dips it into the boiling stock and leaves it there until cooked. He then dips it into his bowl of egg and soy sauce before eating it. When all the raw ingredients have been eaten, the stock is poured into the bowls containing the remains of the egg and soy sauce, stirred around and drunk as soup.

Rice, Noodles and Dumplings

The cookery of North China is famous for its noodle dishes. Noodles are considered a symbol of longevity in China – hence they are nearly all very long. The types usually found in oriental stores in the US are transparent noodles, made of pea-starch or rice powder, and Chinese noodles made of wheat flour. Rice dishes are more common in South China. Long-grain rice is most often used.

Congee

½ cup long-grain rice
1 quart water
1 tablespoon dried shrimps, washed
small piece orange rind

small piece leftover roast pork or duck, finely chopped
½ tablespoon dry sherry
2 tablespoons finely chopped scallion or chives

Put the rice and water in a saucepan. Add the shrimps and orange rind and bring quickly to the boil. Reduce the heat, cover the pan and simmer for 45 minutes. Add the pork or duck and sherry, and simmer gently for another hour. Stir from time to time and add more water if necessary; the rice porridge should not become too thick. Serve in individual bowls, sprinkled with the scallion or chives, as a lunchtime snack.

Special Egg Fried Rice

1½ ounces dried Chinese black mushrooms
½ cup long-grain rice
1 cup frozen peas, thawed and drained
3 ounces canned bamboo shoots, drained and cut into strips
½ pound cold roast chicken, cut into strips

1 cup medium shrimp
4 tablespoons oil
3 ounces canned bean sprouts, drained
3 eggs
4 tablespoons soy sauce
1 tablespoon Chinese rice wine or dry sherry
cayenne pepper
sugar

Soak the mushrooms in warm water for 15 to 30 minutes, until swollen. Drain thoroughly. Meanwhile, bring a pan of salted water to the boil, add the rice and simmer for 10 minutes. Drain the rice, rinse under the cold tap, and drain again thoroughly. Drain the mushrooms. Place the rice in a large bowl and carefully mix in the mushrooms, peas, bamboo shoots, chicken and shrimp.

Heat the oil in a large skillet until very hot. Add the rice mixture and fry, stirring, for 10 minutes. Then add the bean sprouts. Beat the eggs with soy sauce, and rice wine or sherry. Season with a pinch each cayenne pepper and sugar. Pour this mixture over the rice. Allow the eggs to thicken slightly, stirring with a spatula from time to time. Serve immediately.

Special Fried Rice

SPECIAL FRIED RICE

1 cup long-grain rice
½ pound cooked ham
3 tablespoons oil
5 ounces canned shrimp,
   drained

2 tablespoons soy sauce
1 leek, sliced
4 eggs, beaten
salt, pepper

Bring a pan of salted water to the boil. Add the rice and cook at a fast boil for 10 minutes. Drain in a sieve, rinse under the cold tap and drain again. Cut the ham into strips. Heat the oil in a pan. Fry the ham and shrimp for 5 minutes, stirring all the time. Add the rice and soy sauce and fry for another 5 minutes. Add the leek and fry for a further 5 minutes. Season the beaten eggs and stir into the pan until they scramble. Arrange on a warmed plate and serve.

RICE WITH SHRIMP

1 cup long-grain rice
¼ cup butter
9 ounces canned shrimp,
   drained

½ cup white wine
1 teaspoon chopped parsley
salt, pepper

Bring a pan of salted water to the boil, add the rice and simmer for 15 minutes, until tender. Drain, rinse with boiling water and drain again thoroughly. Return the rice to the pan and steam it dry. Set the rice aside.

Melt the butter in a large casserole. Add the shrimp, pour in the wine, and stew gently over low heat for 5 minutes. Mix in the rice and parsley, and season. Bake at 400°F for 15 minutes. Remove from the oven and serve.

INDONESIAN RIJSTAFFEL

Serves 10

This is the famous national dish of Indonesia, served in top-class restaurants all over the world, and highly praised by gourmets. It comes originally from Java. Rijstaffel is a Dutch word meaning, literally, 'rice table'. Because of the number of different dishes involved, it takes quite some time to prepare. For a special meal you should aim for a mixture of 9 or 10 dishes, some hot and some cold. For an ordinary family meal you can serve fewer dishes. All the different dishes are arranged on the table and each guest helps himself to whatever he fancies.

To be served cold:

ROASTED COCONUT

½ cup coconut, coarsely grated	1 teaspoon sugar
¼ cup peanuts	salt

Mix together in a bowl the coconut, peanuts and sugar. Season to taste with salt. Brown in a hot skillet for 5 minutes, stirring all the time. Put into a small bowl for serving.

ROASTED PEANUTS

1 cup peanuts	1 tablespoon coconut oil
salt	

Sprinkle the peanuts with salt. Heat the oil in a skillet, add the peanuts and fry over a moderate heat for 10 minutes, until golden brown. Put into a small bowl for serving.

KROEPOEK

oil for deep frying
1 packet kroepoek

Kroepoek is pounded dried shrimp mixed with tapioca flour, and pressed into dry slices. It can be brought in oriental groceries. The slices are about 1½ inches in size, and swell up to twice that size in the hot fat. Fry only 2 or 3 pieces at a time.

Heat the oil in a large skillet. Deep fry the pieces of kroepoek, 2 or 3 at a time, but do not let them brown or they will lose their flavor. Arrange on a plate for serving.

Note The following should also be served cold. You will need 2 or 3 kinds of sambal (Indonesian relishes made of pounded or crushed ingredients). For instance, sambal oelek (very hot), sambal badjak and sambal goreng. Other suitable accompaniments are small gherkins, sliced cooked beets, small pickled onions, and canned sweet-and-sour ginger. There should also be 1 hard-cooked egg per person, cut into slices, and slices of cold roast chicken. The eggs and chicken slices are covered with a sambal sauce (see below).

SAMBAL SAUCE

½ clove garlic	¼ bay leaf
salt	½ cup tamarind liquid *or*
3 tablespoons coconut oil	½ cup strong chicken stock
1 shallot, chopped	½ cup fresh coconut milk
2 almonds, chopped	sugar
2 small sweet red peppers, seeded and chopped	

Crush the garlic with salt. Heat the oil in a pan, add the shallot, garlic, almonds and peppers, and fry for 5 minutes, until brown. Add the bay leaf, tamarind liquid or chicken stock, and coconut milk. Bring to the boil, stirring, and continue to boil for 1 minute. Season to taste with salt and sugar. Allow to cool. Arrange the hard-cooked egg and chicken slices (see note on page 54) on a plate; pour the sauce over before serving.

Recipe continues over

CURRY SOUP

1 clove garlic	1 teaspoon ground ginger
salt, ground coriander	2 pounds chicken, skinned
3 tablespoons oil	and boned
3 small sweet red peppers,	3 tablespoons butter
seeded and chopped	1 pound canned celery,
3 small green peppers, seeded	drained and chopped
and chopped	1 bay leaf
5 shallots, chopped	1½ quarts hot water
1 teaspoon ground cumin	juice 1 lemon

The original version of this recipe uses an Indian vegetable called seré instead of the celery; you may be able to find it canned in stores specialising in exotic foods.

Crush the garlic with salt. Heat the oil in a pan. Add the peppers, shallots, garlic, cumin and a pinch coriander, and fry gently for a few minutes, stirring. Add the ginger. Fry for 15 minutes, until brown. Put the mixture through a sieve or blender, and put aside. Cut the chicken into pieces about 1½ inches in size. Heat the butter in a large pan, add the chicken and fry gently on all sides for 15 minutes, until browned. Add the celery, bay leaf, reserved purée and water, and simmer for 30 minutes, until the chicken is tender. Season to taste with the lemon juice and salt, remove the bay leaf, and keep warm until needed.

INDIAN CHICKEN CURRY

3 pounds chicken	1 tablespoon lemon juice
¼ cup butter	salt, pepper
1 onion, chopped	2 tablespoons golden raisins
2 teaspoons flour	2 tablespoons blanched
1 teaspoon curry powder	almonds
2 teaspoons curry paste	2 teaspoons shredded coconut
1½ cups chicken stock	2 tablespoons cream
1 apple, peeled and chopped	1 banana, sliced
2 teaspoons mango chutney	

Divide the chicken into neat pieces. Melt the butter in a large pan, add the chicken and fry until lightly browned. Remove from the pan, drain and keep warm. Add the onion and fry until golden. Add the flour, curry powder and curry paste and fry well, stirring occasionally. Stir in the stock and bring to the boil. Return the chicken pieces to the pan and add all the remaining ingredients except the cream and banana. (The coconut should be tied in cheesecloth and removed after 15 minutes.) Simmer gently for 1¼ hours, adding a little more stock if necessary.

Remove the chicken pieces from the pan, drain and keep warm. Stir the cream into the sauce and put aside. Before serving reheat the sauce and pour over the chicken pieces. Garnish with banana slices.

SATCH

Small meat kabobs, prepared according to the recipe for Sate Bali (see page 50). Keep warm until needed.

Recipe continues over

MEAT DUMPLINGS

1 clove garlic	1 onion, chopped
salt	dried mint
1 pound hamburger	¼ cup coconut oil
5 tablespoons cold water	1 cup hot stock
1 teaspoon ground coriander	1 teaspoon curry powder
1 teaspoon ground cumin	1 tablespoon cornstarch

Crush the garlic with salt. Mix the beef and water together in a pan until you have a thick mass. Heat gently for 5 minutes, stirring. Remove from the heat, add the coriander, cumin, onion, garlic and a pinch dried mint, and mix well. Knead into a doughy consistency. Season with salt if desired. Wet the hands and form the mixture into small dumplings ¾ inch across. Heat the coconut oil in a pan, add the dumplings and fry for 10 minutes, until browned. Transfer to a bowl and keep warm.

To make the sauce, add the stock to the remaining oil and meat juices in the pan. Stir in the curry powder. Mix the cornstarch to a smooth paste in a cup with a little cold water. Blend a little of the hot liquid into the mixture, then return to the pan. Bring slowly to the boil, stirring constantly. Simmer for 2 to 3 minutes to allow the flour to cook through. Adjust the seasoning and put aside. Just before serving reheat the sauce and pour over the dumplings.

FRIED SHRIMP

2 cups frozen shrimp, thawed	breadcrumbs
2 egg yolks	5 tablespoons coconut oil

Press the shrimp flat, coat with egg yolk and then with breadcrumbs. Heat the oil in a pan and fry the shrimp for 10 minutes, until brown. Keep warm until needed.

Note You should also serve hot a large bowl of boiled, long-grain rice (2 cups) and a bowl of banana slices fried in butter (use 6 bananas).

INDONESIAN RICE SALAD

½ cup long-grain rice	1 chilli pepper, seeded and chopped
2 tablespoons oil	1 piece preserved stem ginger, chopped
1 onion, finely chopped	
1 tablespoon curry powder	
½ pound cold roast chicken, cut into strips	DRESSING
1 apple, peeled, cored and chopped	juice 1 lemon
	4 tablespoons tomato catsup
1 orange, divided into segments, pith and skin removed, and chopped	1-2 teaspoons Pernod
	4 tablespoons mayonnaise
	2 tablespoons sour cream
1 banana, peeled and chopped	GARNISH
½ fennel bulb, trimmed and chopped	¼ cup flaked almonds, toasted
1 sweet red pepper, seeded and chopped	1 orange, sliced
	8 maraschino cherries

Bring a pan of salted water to the boil. Add the rice, reduce the heat and simmer for 15 minutes, until tender. Drain the rice, rinse under the cold tap, and drain again thoroughly.

Heat the oil in a pan and fry the onion gently for 5 minutes, until soft. Remove the pan from the heat and stir in the curry powder and rice. Turn the contents of the pan into a bowl, and mix in the chicken, fruit, vegetables and ginger.

To make the dressing, mix the lemon juice, tomato catsup, Pernod, mayonnaise and cream in a bowl. Pour three quarters of the dressing on to the rice mixture and mix in thoroughly. Allow to stand for 1 hour.

To serve, arrange the rice salad in 4 separate bowls. Pour the remaining dressing over the 4 salads, and garnish with the nuts, orange slices and cherries

Congee see page 52

Nasi Goreng

Serves 8

1 pound boiling chicken, quartered
1 quart water
salt, pepper
1½ cups long-grain rice
1 sweet red pepper, seeded
½ cup oil
4 onions, chopped
3 cloves garlic, chopped
10 ounces canned crabmeat, drained

½ pound cooked ham
2 cups canned medium shrimp, drained
3 eggs beaten
1 teaspoon sambal oelek (an Indonesian relish)
curry powder, ground ginger, ground cumin, ground coriander, ground nutmeg, powdered saffron (or turmeric)

Place the chicken pieces in a large, heavy saucepan. Cover generously with water and bring to the boil. Skim off any froth or bits which rise to the surface. Reduce the heat and simmer, covered, for 1 hour or until tender.

Remove the chicken pieces from the stock and allow to cool. Then remove the skin and bones from the chicken, cut the flesh into small pieces and set aside. Put the chicken stock in a pan, add the 1 quart water and a pinch salt, and bring to the boil. Meanwhile wash the rice until the water runs clear. Add the rice to the boiling liquid and simmer for 12 minutes over low heat, until the rice grains have swelled but are not completely cooked. Drain in a sieve, pour warm water over the rice to rinse it, and drain again. Cut the pepper into narrow strips.

Heat ⅓ cup of the oil in a large pan. Add the onions, garlic and pepper and stew gently for 5 minutes. Add the rice. Continue cooking very gently for 10 minutes, stirring frequently. Remove any horny strips from the crabmeat. Cut the ham into strips. Add the crabmeat, ham, shrimp and chicken to the pan and mix. Heat the remaining oil in another pan. Add the eggs and scramble, stirring. Mix the sambal oelek and spices to taste in a cup with a little water. Add to the rice mixture with the scrambled egg and stir. Leave over a very low heat for 10 minutes, stirring occasionally. Transfer the mixture to a warmed bowl and serve.

Note Nasi goreng should be served with a selection of spicy sauces and side dishes. These can be prepared beforehand or bought ready-made. Suitable accompaniments would be: sweet peppers in an oil and vinegar dressing; pineapple chunks; pickled cucumber; chilli sauce; mixed pickles; mustard pickles; mango chutney; tomato catsup; soy sauce; fried sliced banana; candied ginger; roasted peanuts or cashew nuts and any Indonesian relish available.

JAVANESE RICE

1 cup long-grain rice
¼ cup butter or margarine
4 chicken legs weighing 1½ pounds altogether, skinned, boned and sliced
2 cups shrimp
2 sweet red peppers, seeded and chopped

1 piece preserved stem ginger
¼ cup flaked almonds
1 teaspoon curry powder
ground ginger
1 small jar (7 ounces) Chinese or Italian fruits pickled with mustard, drained

Wash the rice thoroughly under the cold tap and drain. Bring a pan of salted water to the boil, add the rice and simmer gently for 15 minutes.

Meanwhile melt the butter or margarine in a large pan. Fry the chicken slices on all sides for 5 minutes, until lightly browned. Add the shrimp and peppers and continue frying for another 5 minutes, stirring all the time. Cut the piece of ginger into quarters and then into very thin slices. Add to the pan with the almonds and continue frying for a further 3 minutes. Drain the rice in a sieve, rinse with warm water and drain again. Add the rice to the pan and heat through, stirring. Season with the curry powder and a small pinch ground ginger. Stir in the fruits and serve.

CURRIED PRAWN RICE

2 cups medium shrimp
juice ½ lemon
1 tablespoon raisins
1 cup long-grain rice
2 tablespoons butter
1 onion, chopped

2 teaspoons curry powder
½ cup hot stock
5 tablespoons light cream
pepper
2 tablespoons flaked almonds

Sprinkle the shrimp with the lemon juice, and soak the raisins in hot water. Bring a pan of salted water to the boil, add the rice and simmer for 15 minutes, until tender. Drain, rinse with boiling water, and drain again thoroughly. Keep hot in a bowl in the oven.

Melt 1½ tablespoons of the butter in a pan and fry the onion for 10 minutes, until golden. Stir in the curry powder. Add the stock and bring to the boil, stirring. Boil for 3 minutes. Drain the shrimp and raisins. Remove the pan from the heat and stir in the shrimp and cream. Season with pepper and reheat to just below boiling point. Take the pan off the stove.

Melt the remaining butter in a small skillet and fry the nuts until golden. Stir them into the curry sauce with the raisins. Then stir in the rice, heat through thoroughly and serve.

FAR EASTERN RICE PLATTER

1½ cups long-grain rice
½ cup butter
¼ cup golden raisins
¾ pound pork tenderloin
salt, pepper
4 tablespoons oil
½ pound fillets of sole
5 tablespoons lemon juice
2 cups shrimp
7 ounces canned sweet red
   peppers, drained and
   chopped
1 cup ripe olives, pitted and
   sliced
½ pound fresh mushrooms,
   quartered

2 bananas
1 cup flaked almonds, toasted
1 cup drained pineapple pieces

CURRY SAUCE
¼ cup butter
¼ cup flour
2 cups hot stock
4 tablespoons curry powder
½ cup white wine
salt, pepper
sugar
2 tablespoons light cream

Bring a pan of salted water to the boil, add the rice and boil for 10 minutes, until just tender. Drain, rinse under the cold tap, and drain again thoroughly. Grease a baking sheet with butter and spread the rice out on it. Cut 1 tablespoon of the butter into flakes and arrange them on top of the rice. Bake at 350°F for 15 minutes, until all the moisture has steamed away.

Meanwhile, soak the golden raisins in hot water, and make the curry sauce as follows. Melt the butter in a pan. Add the flour and stir until smooth. Still stirring, add the stock, curry powder and wine. Season with salt, pepper and a pinch sugar. Bring to the boil, remove the pan from the heat, and stir in the cream. Adjust seasoning; keep the sauce hot.

Cut the pork first into thin slices, and then into narrow strips of even size. Season with salt and pepper. Heat 2 tablespoons oil in a pan, and fry the pork strips on all sides for 8 minutes. Remove and keep hot.

Sprinkle the sole fillets with 4 tablespoons of the lemon juice and a little salt. Heat the remaining oil in another pan and fry sole fillets for 5 minutes each side. Then add the shrimp and heat through. Remove and keep hot.

Drain the golden raisins thoroughly. Melt 1½ tablespoons of the butter in a pan. Add the golden raisins, pineapple pieces, red peppers and olives to the pan, and fry gently, stirring, until heated through thoroughly. Remove and keep hot.

Melt 1 tablespoon of the butter in a pan and fry the mushrooms for 10 minutes. Season with the remaining lemon juice, and salt and pepper. Remove and keep hot.

Finally, peel the bananas, cut each in half widthways, and then cut each piece in half lengthways. Melt the remaining butter in a pan, and fry the banana pieces frequently and baste them with the butter in the pan.

Now assemble the dish. Spread the rice out on a large, flat serving plate. Arrange the pork, the sole and shrimp mixture, the golden raisin, pineapple, pepper and olive mixture, the mushrooms, and the fried bananas on top of the rice. Scatter on the nuts and serve. Hand the curry sauce separately.

SUKIYAKI

½ pound transparent noodles
½ ounce dried Chinese black
  mushrooms
1½ pounds sirloin steak,
  thinly sliced
3 tablespoons shortening
2 cups long-grain rice
4 onions
4 leeks
½ pound white cabbage
1 pound canned bamboo
  shoots
½ pound spinach, washed
  and picked over

½ pound fresh bean sprouts,
  cleaned or ½ pound canned
  bean sprouts, drained
4 egg yolks

SAUCE
1 cup shoyu sauce or 1 cup soy
  sauce
⅓ cup sake
2 teaspoons sugar

Put the noodles and black mushrooms into separate bowls. Pour on boiling water and leave to soak and swell up for 20 minutes, changing the water twice. Arrange the slices of meat on a dish like petals, with the lump of shortening in the center. Cover with aluminum foil and place in the refrigerator until required.

Bring a pan of salted water to the boil, add the rice and simmer for 15 minutes, until tender. Meanwhile cut the onions and leeks into rings. Cut out the cabbage stalk, take the leaves apart and wash and drain them. Halve or quarter the larger leaves. Drain the bamboo shoots, reserving their liquid. Cut into thin slices. Drain the noodles and black mushrooms. Arrange all the raw ingredients, including the meat, round the broiler on the table in individual bowls or plates.

To make the sauce, bring the shoyu or soy sauce to the boil in a pan with the sake, sugar and 4 tablespoons of the reserved bamboo shoot liquid. Put in a bowl and place on the table. Drain the rice, rinse with boiling water, drain again and place on the table in a bowl.

Sukiyaki is cooked in the following way. Rub round the inside of the cooking pan with the piece of shortening. Set it over the heat, add a quarter of the meat and fry quickly, stirring. Push the meat to one side of the pan and pour some of the sauce over it. Add a quarter of all the remaining ingredients (except the rice and egg) and fry gently, stirring, for 3 minutes. The meat and vegetables are then divided between the guests; the cooked vegetables are dipped in the egg yolk before being eaten. While the first portion of meat and vegetables is being eaten the second is being prepared in the same way, and so on until all the ingredients have been cooked. Each guest seasons his food to taste with the sauce and helps himself to rice.

It is a good idea to take turns over the cooking, to avoid having one person always attending to the pan. Green tea is the correct drink to accompany sukiyaki with a cup or bowl of warm sake afterwards.

BAMI KUAH

½ pound Chinese egg
noodles
3½ tablespoons oil
½ chicken (1½ pounds)
½ pound pork
salt, pepper
1 quart water
2 ounces fresh button
mushrooms
1 clove garlic, crushed

1 teaspoon finely chopped
root ginger or ½ teaspoon
ground ginger
1 small leek, sliced
1 tablespoon finely chopped
celery
1 tablespoon soy sauce
3 tablespoons crisply fried
onions
3 tablespoons chopped chives

Cook the noodles until tender as indicated on the package. Drain in a sieve, rinse under the cold tap and drain again thoroughly. Then turn them in ½ tablespoon of the oil. Put the chicken and pork in a saucepan and season. Add the water and bring to the boil. Skim the liquid, reduce the heat, cover the pan and leave to simmer for 15 to 20 minutes. Remove the chicken and pork from the saucepan, skin and bone the chicken, and then slice both the chicken and pork thinly. Strain the stock and keep hot.

Heat 2 tablespoons of the oil in a pan and fry the mushrooms for 1 minute. Add the chicken and pork and turn in the hot fat for a further minute. Remove everything from the pan and keep hot. Heat the remaining oil in the pan and fry the garlic and ginger for 1 minute. Remove and add to the other ingredients being kept hot. Then fry the leek and celery in the fat for 2 to 3 minutes. Return the chicken, pork, mushrooms, garlic and ginger to the pan, pour over the hot stock and soy sauce. Add a little more salt to taste. Stir in the noodles and heat through. Serve in large bowls garnished with the onions and chives.

BAMI GORENG

1 pound Chinese noodles
3–4 tablespoons oil
2 red onions, finely chopped
1 small leek, sliced
1 clove garlic, crushed
¾ pound roast pork,
chopped
1 teaspoon finely chopped
root ginger or ½ teaspoon
ground ginger
salt, pepper
4 scallions, chopped

1 tablespoon finely chopped
celery
2 cups shrimp
1 tablespoon soy sauce
2 tablespoons chicken or
other stock
1 tablespoon crisply fried
onions
½ tablespoon finely chopped
parsley
2 eggs, beaten

Cook the noodles as indicated on the package. Drain in a sieve, rinse under the cold tap and drain again thoroughly. Then turn in ½ tablespoon of the oil.

Heat 2 to 3 tablespoons of the remaining oil in a large skillet. Add the red onions, leek and garlic, and fry until golden brown. Add the meat and ginger, season, and fry together, stirring, for a few minutes. Add the scallions, celery and shrimp, and fry for a further 1 to 1½ minutes over medium heat. After adding a little more oil if necessary, put the noodles in the pan. Fry over high heat, stirring constantly, for 2 minutes, or until they are fully heated through and lightly fried. Stir in the soy sauce and stock. Transfer to a warmed bowl, garnish with the onions and parsley, and keep hot.

Quickly cook a thin omelet with the eggs. Cut the omelet into ½ inch strips, make a lattice pattern over the noodles and serve.

CHOP SUEY

1 pound lean pork
2 tablespoons Chinese rice
  wine or dry sherry
4 tablespoons soy sauce
salt, pepper, ground ginger
2 ounces transparent noodles
2 ounces celery
1 tablespoon dried Chinese
  black mushrooms
3 ounces canned bamboo
  shoots, drained

½ cup coconut oil
2 onions, chopped
5 ounces canned bean
  sprouts, drained
¼ pound fresh mushrooms,
  sliced
1 teaspoon sugar
1½ tablespoons cornstarch
¼ cup dry sherry

Cut the pork into thin strips. Mix the rice wine or sherry and 2 tablespoons soy sauce in a bowl. Season with salt, pepper and a pinch ground ginger. Add the pork strips to the marinade, cover and allow to stand for 1 hour. Meanwhile break up the noodles into small pieces. Bring a pan of lightly salted water to the boil, add the noodles and simmer for 5 minutes. Rinse under the cold tap, drain and put aside. Cut the celery into short strips and blanch for 5 minutes in boiling, lightly salted water. Remove and drain. Soak the dried black mushrooms in warm water for 30 minutes, drain and cut into fairly large pieces. Cut the bamboo shoots into strips.

Put the oil in a large skillet and heat it until very hot. Remove the pork from the marinade, drain well and fry in the oil for 2 minutes. Remove and keep warm. Add the onions, bamboo shoots, bean sprouts, black mushrooms and fresh mushrooms. Fry for 3 minutes. Mix in the pork, celery and noodles. Season with the remaining soy sauce and the sugar. Simmer for another 3 minutes, stirring gently.

Mix the cornstarch to a smooth paste in a cup with the sherry. Add to the pan and bring slowly to the boil, stirring constantly. Simmer for 2 to 3 minutes to allow the flour to cook through. Adjust the seasoning and serve at once with boiled, long-grain rice.

FRIED NOODLES WITH PORK

½ pound pork tenderloin
½ cup soy sauce
4 tablespoons Chinese rice
  wine or dry sherry
½ pound Chinese noodles
½ cup coconut oil
⅓ ounce dried Chinese
  mushrooms

¼ pound leek
½ pound canned bamboo
  shoots, drained
¼ pound cooked ham
salt
1 teaspoon mild paprika
ground ginger

Slice the pork thinly against the grain of the meat. Cut the slices into strips and place in a bowl. Mix together 2 tablespoons each of the soy sauce and rice wine or sherry. Pour over the meat and leave to marinate for 30 minutes, turning from time to time.

Meanwhile, bring a pan of salted water to the boil, add the noodles and cook at a fast boil for 3 to 4 minutes. They should be tender but not quite cooked. Rinse in a sieve under the cold tap and drain. Place in a warmed bowl with 1 tablespoon of the oil. Keep warm. Break up the mushrooms slightly, pour boiling water over them and leave to soak for 10 minutes. Meanwhile cut the leek into halves or quarters, according to its thickness, then cut into strips 1¼ inches long. Cut the bamboo shoots and ham into similar-sized strips. Remove the mushrooms from the water and drain.

Heat 3 tablespoons of the oil in a large skillet. Remove the pork strips from the marinade, reserving the marinade. Drain the pork and add to the hot oil. Fry briefly, stirring so that the meat does not stick. Add the leek, bamboo shoots, ham and mushrooms. Fry for 4 minutes, stirring. Pour in the reserved marinade and bring to the boil. Remove from the heat immediately, transfer to a warmed bowl and keep warm.

Clean out the skillet. Heat the remaining oil, add the noodles and fry for 10 minutes. Season lightly with salt. Mix together the paprika, a pinch ground ginger and the remaining soy sauce and rice wine or sherry. Pour this mixture over the noodles, mix well and fry for another minute. To serve, arrange the noodles in the center of a warmed bowl and place the meat and vegetables around them.

CHICKEN WITH FRIED NOODLES

3 pound chicken
5 tablespoons oil
salt, pepper
sugar
10 ounces canned celery, drained and chopped
10 ounces water chestnuts, drained and chopped
¼ pound canned mushrooms, drained and sliced

5 tablespoons soy sauce
1 teaspoon cornstarch
2 eggs
3 tablespoons water
½ pound Chinese noodles
3 tablespoons shortening
2 scallions, sliced
   or 1 tablespoon chopped chives

Bring a large pan of lightly salted water to the boil. Add the chicken and simmer for 1½ hours, until tender. Remove from the pan, reserving the stock. Remove the chicken skin, take the meat off the bones and cut it into small pieces.

Heat 3 tablespoons of the oil in a skillet. Fry the chicken pieces for 5 minutes until browned on all sides. Season with salt, pepper and sugar to taste. Add ½ cup of the reserved hot stock. Add the celery, water chestnuts and mushrooms to the pan and simmer for 5 minutes over low heat. Add the soy sauce. Mix the cornstarch to a smooth paste with a little cold water in a cup. Blend a little of the hot liquid into the mixture, then return to the pan. Bring slowly to the boil, stirring constantly. Simmer for 2 to 3 minutes to allow the flour to cook through. Remove from the heat and keep warm.

Mix the eggs in a bowl with the water and flour. Season with salt and pepper. Heat the remaining oil in a skillet. Use the batter to make 4 thin crepes, cooking them 2 minutes each side. Cut into narrow strips and keep warm.

Bring a pan of salted water to the boil, add the noodles and simmer for 20 minutes until tender. Drain in a sieve, rinse with cold water and drain again. Heat the shortening in a pan and fry the noodles for 10 minutes until golden brown. Drain on absorbent paper.

Put the noodles into a warm bowl and pour the chicken and vegetables over them. Arrange the crepe strips on top and serve garnished with the scallions or chives.

CHICKEN CHOW MEIN

1 small green pepper, seeded
1 small sweet red pepper, seeded
3 tablespoons butter
1 small onion, chopped
2 stalks celery, chopped
1½ tablespoons flour
1 cup hot chicken stock (see page 7)
2 tablespoons soy sauce
pepper

5 ounces canned mushrooms, drained and sliced
½ pound cooked chicken breast, chopped
½ pound broad Chinese noodles
oil for frying
½ cup flaked almonds, fried in butter and salted

Cut the peppers into thin strips and blanch in boiling water for 5 minutes. Remove and drain. Melt 2 tablespoons of the butter in a pan, add the onion and celery, and fry lightly for 2 minutes. Sprinkle the flour over, add the stock, bring to the boil and simmer for 10 minutes, until the vegetables are just tender. Season with the soy sauce and pepper. Add the pepper strips, mushrooms and chicken breast. Cover the pan and simmer, gently, for 15 minutes.

Bring a pan of salted water to the boil, add the noodles and simmer for 15 minutes. Drain, rinse with cold water and drain again. Set aside one third of the noodles. Add the remaining butter to the rest and put into a warmed serving bowl. Cover and keep warm.

Cut the remaining noodles, which must be very well drained, into pieces. Heat the oil in a skillet and fry the noodles until golden yellow. Drain on absorbent paper. Pour the chicken sauce over the buttered noodles and sprinkle the fried noodles and salted almonds on top. Alternatively, the chicken sauce, buttered noodles, fried noodles and salted almonds can all be served separately.

Chicken Chow Mein

JO CHON BAU

1 pound pork scallops
2 onions
1 leek
¼ cup butter
salt

FIRST MARINADE
4 tablespoons tomato catsup
1 tablespoon vinegar
1 teaspoon mild paprika
3 drops Tabasco sauce
1 teaspoon curry powder

SECOND MARINADE
½ cup soy sauce
1 tablespoon dry sherry
1 tablespoon honey
ground ginger

DOUGH
¾ ounce fresh yeast *or* 1
  tablespoon dried yeast
1 teaspoon sugar
1 cup warm water
3½ cups flour
½ teaspoon salt

Pat the pork scallops dry with absorbent paper. Trim off any fat.

To make the first marinade, mix together the tomato catsup, vinegar, paprika. Tabasco sauce and curry powder. Put the meat in a bowl, cover with the marinade, and leave for 10 minutes to absorb the flavors. Meanwhile brush the broiler rack with oil and put the broiler pan underneath to catch any drips. Remove the scallops from the marinade, drain and grill for 10 minutes each side. Alternatively fry the meat in a little oil, over gentle heat, for 10 minutes each side.

While the meat is cooking prepare the second marinade: warm the soy sauce and sherry in a saucepan. Add the honey and stir until dissolved. Season with a pinch ground ginger and take the pan off the heat. Remove the pork scallops from the broiler or skillet, cut into cubes ½ inch square, and add to the pan. Cover and leave to stand for 45 minutes.

To make the dough, mix the fresh yeast with the sugar and a little of the water, then add the remaining water. (If using dried yeast, dissolve the sugar in the water, sprinkle on the yeast and stir well.) Leave to stand in a warm place for about 10 minutes.

Meanwhile, sift the flour and salt into a bowl. Make a well in the center and pour in the yeast mixture. Working from the outside in, knead to a soft dough which leaves the sides of the bowl clean (about 10 minutes). Add a little more flour if necessary. Allow the dough to stand in a warm place, covered with a clean cloth, until it doubles in size.

Meanwhile cut the onions into strips. Cut the leek in half lengthways, wash and drain, and cut into pieces ¼ inch long. Then heat 2 tablespoons for the butter in a skillet, add the onions and leek pieces and fry for 5 minutes, stirring. Remove the pieces of meat from the second marinade, drain and add to the pan. Season with salt and stew all together for 5 minutes.

Turn the dough on to a floured surface. Knead again for 1 to 2 minutes to knock out air bubbles. Then roll out and divide into 8 portions. Form each portion into a circular shape with your hands, put some of the meat mixture into the center of each circle, and fold the dough into parcels, pressing the edges well together. Melt the remaining butter and paint it over the dough parcels. Cover a roasting grid with foil, grease the foil with margarine, and place the dough parcels on it. Place the grid on a roasting pan partly filled with water. Roast for 20 minutes at 475°F. Remove from the oven and serve.

CHINESE STEAMED ROLLS

½ ounce fresh yeast or 2
  teaspoons dried yeast
2 tablespoons sugar
1 cup warm water
4 cups flour
2 tablespoons oil
4 scallions chopped *or* ½
  onion, chopped

1 clove garlic, crushed
1 pound Chinese roast fat
  back (see page 38), finely
  shredded.
2 tablespoons soy sauce
½ tablespoon dry sherry
1½ tablespoons cornstarch
3 tablespoons water or stock

To make the dough, mix the fresh yeast with the sugar and a little of the water, then add the remaining water. (If using dried yeast, dissolve the sugar in the water, sprinkle on the yeast and stir well.) Leave to stand in a warm place for about 10 minutes.

Meanwhile sift the flour into a bowl. Make a well in the center and pour in the yeast mixture. Working from the outside in, knead to a soft dough which leaves the sides of the bowl clean (about 10 minutes). Add a little more flour if necessary. Allow the dough to stand in a warm place, covered with a clean cloth, until it has doubled in size.

Meanwhile make the filling. Heat the oil in a pan. Add the onion and garlic and fry until golden. Add the pork and stir over high heat until thoroughly heated through. Add the soy sauce, sherry and remaining sugar and mix in well. Mix the cornstarch to a smooth paste in a cup with the water or stock.

Stir into the ingredients in the pan until the sauce is thick and shiny. Remove the pan from the heat and allow to cool.

Turn the dough onto a floured surface. Knead again for 1 to 2 minutes to knock out air bubbles. Shape into a sausage 2 inches thick, and cut into slices ¾ inch thick. Roll these slices out until they are 3–4 inches across. Divide the filling among the dough slices, heaping it up in the center. Fold the edges upwards so that the filling is completely enclosed, and shape into a ball. Cut circles of aluminum foil or wax paper just large enough for the rolls to stand on. Place each roll on a circle inside a steamer, over a pan of boiling water. Steam the rolls ¾ inch apart, a few at a time, for 15 to 20 minutes, or until the topsides are shiny and firm. These rolls can be eaten either hot or cold.

SIU MAI

Serves 8–10

3 dried Chinese mushrooms
¾ pound lean pork, chopped
¼ pound fat ham, chopped
1 frozen Jumbo shrimp, thawed and chopped
1 walnut-sized piece bamboo, chopped
2 water chestnuts (optional), chopped
1 tablespoon sake, Chinese rice wine or dry sherry
1 teaspoon soy sauce
few drops sesame oil
½ teaspoon sugar
1 egg white, beaten
salt, pepper
10 egg or spring roll skins

Soak the mushrooms in hot water for 15 to 30 minutes, until swollen. Squeeze them dry, remove the stems and cut the caps into short, thin strips. Mix together all the ingredients except the egg roll skins, and set the mixture aside for 1 hour.

Meanwhile take the egg roll skins one at a time, and cut out 4 circles of 4 inches diameter from each; use a pastry cutter or saucer of the right diameter. Divide the filling into 40 equal portions and shape into balls. Place each on a circle of dough. Fold the edges upward over the filling and crimp carefully together. Hold the dumpling a little way above a pastry board and let it drop a few times to flatten the underside and settle the filling. There must be no air between the filling and the dough case. Continue in this way until all the dumplings have been shaped, keeping the egg roll skins and the completed dumplings covered with polythene sheets as you work.

Steam the dumplings for 20 to 30 minutes. Place a small piece of aluminum foil under each dumpling to prevent sticking to the bottom of the steamer. If you only have a small steamer, the dumplings can be steamed in batches, then all heated up together before serving. Serve as an hors d'oeuvre or lunch dish, with an accompanying dip of chilli sauce.

Siu Mai

EGG DISHES

JAPANESE EGG SALAD

7 ounces canned tuna,
  drained
7 ounces canned mandarin
  oranges, drained
4 hard-cooked eggs, sliced
1/4 cup stuffed olives,
  sliced

2 tablespoons oil
juice 1 lemon
2 tablespoons soy sauce
salt, pepper
sugar
sprigs parsley

Flake the fish into a bowl. Add the mandarin oranges, eggs and olives and mix together lightly. To make the dressing, mix together the oil, lemon juice and soy sauce. Season to taste with salt, pepper and pinch sugar. Pour over the salad. Stand the salad in the refrigerator, covered, for 10 minutes to absorb the flavors. To serve, divide the salad between four glass bowls and garnish each with a sprig of parsley.

CHINESE TEA EGGS

Makes 6

2 quarts water
2 tablespoons jasmine tea

1/2 cup sugar
6 hard-cooked eggs
  (unshelled)

Bring the water to the boil in a pan. Add the tea and sugar, and continue to boil for 15 minutes. Strain the liquid, bring back to the boil and allow to simmer gently for 1 hour. Tap the egg shells on all sides to crack evenly, but do not shell them. Put them in the tea and simmer gently for another hour. Then take the eggs out of the tea and remove the shells. The egg whites will have an attractive marbled appearance. Serve either hot or cold.

CRAWFISH FU YUNG

juice ½ lemon
¼ pound fresh mushrooms, sliced
2 egg whites
1 teaspoon strong chicken stock
salt, pepper
½ cup oil
11 ounces canned crawfish, drained

¼ pound canned bamboo shoots, drained and thinly sliced
1 teaspoon cornstarch
1 tablespoon water
1 teaspoon soy sauce
2 tablespoons Chinese rice wine or dry sherry
½ cup cooked ham, diced

Bring a pan of salted water to the boil. Add the lemon juice and mushrooms and simmer for 5 minutes, until tender. Drain and keep warm.

Mix the egg whites and stock together; season with salt and pepper. Heat the oil in a pan without letting it get too hot. Add the egg white mixture and let it solidify to a smooth, soft consistency. Tip into a sieve and reserve the oil. Pour 3 tablespoons oil back into the pan and reheat. Remove any horny strips from the crawfish and add the crawfish to the pan with the mushrooms and bamboo shoots. Season with salt and pepper and fry for 2 minutes. Then mix in the egg white mixture. Separately, mix the cornstarch, water, soy sauce and rice wine or sherry together. Add to the pan and fry over high heat for 30 seconds. Transfer to a warmed bowl and garnish with the ham.

FU YUNG HAY

2 cloves garlic
salt, pepper, ground ginger
½ cup oil
¾ pound tomatoes, skinned, seeded and chopped
1 teaspoon sugar
2 tablespoons soy sauce
5 ounces frozen snow peas

butter
1 leek, thinly sliced
2 onions, thinly sliced
8 small, tender stalks celery, thinly sliced
8 eggs, beaten
10 ounces canned crawfish tails, drained

To make the tomato sauce, crush the garlic with salt. Heat 2 tablespoons oil in a pan and fry the garlic for 2 minutes, until pale yellow. Add the tomatoes and stew, stirring, until you have a thick sauce. Season with the sugar, soy sauce and a small pinch ground ginger, and keep warm.

Bring a pan of salted water to the boil, add the peas, cover, and simmer for 5 minutes until done. Drain the peas, add a knob of butter and keep warm.

To make the omelets, heat 2 tablespoons oil in a pan. Add the leek, onions and celery and fry for 5 minutes, stirring. Then stir the vegetable mixture into the eggs. Remove any horny strips from the crawfish tails, then stir the tails into the eggs. Season to taste. For each omelet, put 1 tablespoon of the remaining oil in a skillet. Heat until it is smoking and ladle in a quarter of the egg mixture. Fry over low heat for 5 minutes, shaking the pan from time to time. The omelets should be cooked in quick succession, slide onto warm plates and kept hot. When all the omelets have been cooked, scatter the peas round the edge and serve at once. Hand the tomato sauce separately.

VEGETABLES

BEBOTOK

1 pound hamburger
2 tablespoons finely chopped
  onion
1 clove garlic, crushed
1 chilli pepper, shredded *or* ½
  teaspoon chilli sauce
1½ tablespoons ground
  coriander
½ tablespoon ground cumin
6 blanched almonds, chopped
½ teaspoon galingale
  (optional)
½ teaspoon soft brown sugar
3 tablespoons grated coconut
  (preferably fresh)
½ teaspoon belacan (shrimp
  paste)
1 teaspoon salt
1 egg, lightly beaten
8–10 large, white or green
  cabbage leaves

Put all the ingredients except the cabbage leaves into a large bowl, and work together until the mixture becomes tacky and sticks together. Add a little milk if the mixture is too dry. Divide the mixture into 8 to 10 equal portions, forming each into a slightly flattened ball. Bring a pan of water to the boil, add the cabbage leaves, and simmer until they are soft enough to be folded without breaking. Rinse and drain well. Lay one portion of the filling on each of the leaves, fold the leaves up into a package and secure with toothpicks

Place the rolls in a steamer over a pan of boiling water. Steam the rolls for 20 to 25 minutes with the lid on, until cooked. Remove from the steamer and serve.

CHINESE MUSHROOMS

1 ounce dried Chinese black
  mushrooms
3 tablespoons soy sauce
1 tablespoon Chinese rice
  wine or dry sherry
1 teaspoon sugar
1 tablespoon cornstarch
½ pound lean ground pork
4 canned water chestnuts,
  drained and chopped
salt
2 tablespoons oil
sprigs parsley

Soak the mushrooms in warm water for 15 to 30 minutes, until swollen. Drain in a sieve, reserving the water. Cut off and discard any stems. To make the stuffing, mix together in a bowl 1 tablespoon of the soy sauce, the rice wine or sherry, sugar and cornstarch. Stir in the pork and water chestnuts, and season with salt.

Heat the oil in a large skillet. Place the mushrooms in the pan, rounded side downwards. Divide the stuffing between the mushrooms and spread it flat with a knife. Fry the mushrooms over moderate heat for 1 minute, until the undersides are slightly browned. Pour 4 tablespoons of the reserved soaking water into the pan, bring to the boil, cover the pan, and stew for 15 minutes over very low heat.

Remove the mushrooms carefully from the pan with a perforated spoon, and arrange on a warmed bowl, stuffed side up. Add the remaining soy sauce to the pan and reheat the liquid, stirring. Pour the sauce over the mushrooms, garnish with the parsley and serve.

Note If you cannot get dried Chinese black mushrooms, use large, flat, fresh mushrooms.

CHINESE CABBAGE

2 Chinese cabbages   grated nutmeg
1½ tablespoons butter

Shred the cabbage leaves, cut them into finger-length pieces, or leave them whole, according to taste. Wash and drain. Bring a pan of salted water to the boil, add the cabbage and simmer for 20 to 25 minutes, until tender. (The quicker it is cooked the better.) Drain and return to the pan. Add the butter and shake over gentle heat until the butter has melted and the cabbage is coated. Sprinkle with grated nutmeg and serve.

BRAISED CHINESE CABBAGE

2 Chinese cabbages,   1 cup stock
  quartered   1-2 tablespoons soy sauce
salt   1 tablespoon chopped parsley
¼ cup bacon,
  chopped
1 onion, chopped

Season the cabbages lightly with salt. Melt the bacon in a pan until the fat runs. Add the onion and brown slightly. Add the cabbage and fry quickly, but do not allow to brown. Pour the stock into the pan and simmer for 20 minutes, until the cabbage is tender. Season with soy sauce and more salt if necessary. Transfer to a warmed bowl and serve garnished with parsley.

CHINESE MIXED VEGETABLES

⅓ ounce dried Chinese black   4 tablespoons sesame seed oil
  mushrooms   ½ cup frozen peas
¼ pound white cabbage   ½ cup hot chicken
¼ pound carrots, peeled   stock (see page 7)
1 cucumber, peeled
¼ pound canned bamboo
  shoots, drained

Soak the mushrooms in warm water for 15 to 30 minutes, until swollen. Meanwhile cut the cabbage, carrots, cucumber and bamboo shoots into conveniently-sized strips. Drain the mushrooms and cut into pieces. Heat the oil in a skillet and fry the cabbage, stirring, for 2 minutes. Stir in the mushrooms, carrots. cucumber, bamboo shoots and peas and heat through. Add the stock. Season with the soy sauce and a pinch of salt and sugar. Simmer over low heat for 15 minutes, stirring occasionally. Serve at once.

Chinese Mixed Vegetables

CHINESE CABBAGE, STIR-FRIED

1 dried Chinese mushroom	½ cup chicken stock
2 Chinese cabbages	(see page 7)
2 tablespoons oil	¼ teaspoon sugar
½ tablespoon salt	1 tablespoon soy sauce
1 small piece root ginger,	2 teaspoons cornstarch
finely chopped	1 tablespoon water

Soak the mushroom in hot water for 15 to 30 minutes, until swollen. Drain well, remove the stem and cut the cap into long, thin strips. Cut off the thick stem from the cabbage. Wash the leaves and shred them into fairly short pieces.

Heat the oil in a wok, or other lidded, heavy pan. Add the salt and ginger, and turn in the oil over high heat for 30 seconds. Add the cabbage and mushroom and fry, turning over continuously, for 1½ minutes. Add the stock, sugar and soy sauce, reduce the heat slightly, place the lid on the pan, and let the ingredients simmer gently for 2 minutes. Meanwhile mix the cornstarch to a smooth paste with the water. Then stir this solution into the pan until the sauce thickens and becomes shiny. Serve as an accompaniment to Chinese roast fat back (see page 38), or other meat dishes.

CHINESE STUFFED MUSHROOMS

8 dried Chinese mushrooms	1 tablespoon finely chopped
4-6 ounces lean ground pork	bamboo shoots *or*
1 tablespoon chopped onion	1 tablespoon finely
1 small piece root ginger,	chopped water chestnuts
finely chopped	½ tablespoon soy sauce
	½ tablespoon dry sherry
	½ teaspoon oil
	1 tablespoon chopped parsley

Make sure the mushrooms are large and unbroken. Soak the mushrooms in hot water for 15 to 30 minutes, until swollen. Drain well and remove the stems. Mix together the pork, the onion, ginger, bamboo shoots or water chestnuts, soy sauce, sherry and oil. Fill the mushroom caps with this mixture, pressing down firmly. Place them close together on a dinner plate, cover loosely with a sheet of aluminum foil and steam for 30 minutes, with the lid on. Transfer to a warm bowl, sprinkle with the parsley and serve as an hors d'oeuvre to a Chinese meal.

Note If you cannot get dried Chinese mushrooms, use large, flat, fresh mushrooms.

LEEKS IN BATTER

8 thin leeks
1 tablespoon oil
2 tablespoons soy sauce
1 tablespoon lemon juice
salt, pepper, grated nutmeg
sugar
flour for coating
1 egg
oil for deep frying

Remove all green parts from the leeks and wash thoroughly in cold water. Drain and cut diagonally across into pieces 2–3 inches long. Bring a pan of salted water to the boil, and stir in the 1 tablespoon oil. Add the pieces of leek. Cover the pan, reduce the heat and simmer until the leeks are tender (about 10 minutes).

Meanwhile make the dipping sauce. Mix together the soy sauce and lemon juice. Season with salt, pepper and a pinch sugar. Put the sauce into a jug.

Put the flour on a plate. Break the egg into a bowl and beat it. Remove the leeks from the pan, drain and season with grated nutmeg. Then roll them in the flour, dip in the egg, and deep fry them for 2 minutes, until crisp and golden brown. Remove and drain on absorbent paper, place on a warmed plate and serve at once. Hand the dipping sauce separately.

CHINESE CAULIFLOWER

2 tablespoons oil
1 small cauliflower, broken
  into florets
½ pound lean pork, cubed
1 onion, chopped
2 tablespoons soy sauce
salt
1 cup stock
7 ounces ribbon noodles
1 teaspoon cornstarch
chopped chives

Heat 1 tablespoon of the oil in a large skillet. Add the cauliflower and meat and fry for 2 to 3 minutes, over medium heat, until lightly browned. Add the onion and soy sauce, season with salt, and fry quickly until the onion is golden. Pour in the stock, bring to the boil, reduce the heat and simmer until tender (about 35 minutes).

Meanwhile, bring a pan of salted water to the boil. Add the noodles, reduce the heat and simmer for 10 minutes, until tender. Drain in a sieve, rinse with warm water, and drain again thoroughly. Heat the remaining oil in a skillet. Add the noodles and fry until golden brown. Remove from the pan and drain on absorbent paper.

Mix the cornstarch to a smooth paste with a little cold water in a cup. Blend a little of the hot liquid from the cauliflower and meat into the mixture, then return to the pan. Bring slowly to the boil, stirring constantly. Simmer for 2 to 3 minutes to allow the flour to cook through. Then add the fried noodles and heat through. Transfer to a warmed bowl, garnish with a little chopped chives and serve immediately.

BAMBOO SHOOT SALAD

1 clove garlic
salt, ground ginger
2 tablespoons soy sauce
3 tablespoons vinegar
2 tablespoons oil
2 hard-cooked eggs, chopped
1 sweet red pepper, seeded
  and chopped
sugar
9 ounces canned bamboo
  shoots, drained and sliced
½ sweet pickled cucumber
¼ cooked celeriac root
1 tablespoon chopped
  tarragon
1 tablespoon chopped dill

Crush the garlic with salt. Stir together a pinch of ground ginger, the soy sauce, vinegar and oil to make a smooth dressing. Mix together the eggs and pepper and season with salt and sugar. Then mix with the dressing and stand in the refrigerator for 20 minutes. Mix together the bamboo shoots, cucumber and celeriac. Pour the chilled dressing over the vegetables and mix carefully. Garnish with the chopped herbs and serve.

CHINESE SCALLION TASSELS

scallions, as required

These decorations are always made from scallions, even though they are sometimes referred to as shallot tassels. In Chinese cooking they are used as an edible garnish with many dishes.

Trim off the root as closely as possible. Cut away all except 3 inches of the green stem. With a very sharp knife, cut down the green stem to a depth of ¾–1 inch, and then make a second cut at right angles to it. Bend the four strips out slightly. Place the onions in a bowl of iced water, containing a few ice cubes, until the ends curl over. The same effect can be obtained by moistening the onions, and then putting them in the frozen-food compartment of a refrigerator, again just until the ends curl over.

Desserts

Korean Caramelised Bananas

4 bananas, peeled
2 tablespoons cornstarch
2 egg whites, beaten
flour for coating
oil for deep frying

1 tablespoon butter
½ cup sugar
2 tablespoons water
2 tablespoons sesame seeds

Cut the bananas into pieces ¾ inch long. Mix the cornstarch into the egg whites. Sprinkle some flour on a plate. Dip the banana pieces first in the flour, then in the egg white mixture, and deep fry them until golden brown. Remove and drain on absorbent paper.

To make the sauce, gently heat the butter and sugar in a pan until golden brown. Stir in the water and sesame seeds. Add the fried banana pieces and turn carefully in the sauce. Transfer to a warmed and greased bowl and serve.

Korean Caramelised Bananas

CHINESE HONEY APPLES

2 eggs
½ cup flour
½ cup water
salt

4 dessert apples, peeled
4 tablespoons oil
4 tablespoons honey
4 tablespoons groundnut oil

To make the batter, mix together the eggs, flour, water and a pinch salt in a bowl. Remove the apple cores with an apple corer; cut the apples into thick rounds. Heat the first quantity of oil in a frying pan. Dip the apple rings into the batter, then fry them in the hot oil for 3 minutes each side, until golden brown. Heat the honey and groundnut oil in a pan. Dip the fried apple rings in this mixture and allow to cool.

Note In China a bowl of water with ice cubes is served with this dessert. The freshly-fried apple rings are speared on chopsticks and dipped into the water so that the honey crystallises.

PEKING DUST

1 pound unsweetened, canned chestnut purée
½ cup water
1 cup whipping cream
3 tablespoons caster sugar
1 teaspoon vanilla sugar

1 tablespoons soft dark brown sugar
½ cup granulated sugar
mandarin orange segments, blanched almonds, walnuts and candied cherries to decorate

Mix together in a bowl the chestnut purée and ⅓ cup of the water. Put the cream in another bowl and beat until it begins to thicken. Add the caster sugar and vanilla sugar and beat the cream until stiff. Remove half of the cream from the bowl and blend it into the chestnut purée mixture with the brown sugar. Bring the remaining water and the white sugar to the boil in a pan. Boil, stirring constantly, until a thick syrup is formed.

Dip the fruits and nuts (use as many as or as few as you wish) into this syrup, and then leave them to cool and harden on a piece of wax paper. Put the chestnut purée mixture in a pastry bag. Using a tip with a small round opening, (i.e. not notched), squeeze the mixture out in small lengths and heap them up on a plate. Cover with the remaining whipped cream and decorate with the candied fruits and nuts.

LYCHEES

Lychees, popular as they are in the U.S.A., originally come from China. The fruits are almost round, have a scaly red skin, and grow in clusters on trees about 30 feet high. They have been popular in China since ancient times. Their flesh is firm and white and their flavor is slightly reminiscent of cherries, with a touch of nutmeg. Nowadays canned lychees are available in oriental food shops and are on the menu of every Chinese restaurant.

Today lychees are also grown in South Africa, India, Australia, Hawaii, Brazil and Florida. Hong Kong is the main source of canned lychees. These are preserved in syrup. The Chinese almost always eat the fruit cooked, or dried; hence another name for the lychee is Chinese hazelnut. Lychees are also a rich source of Vitamin C.

PEKING PEARS

4 ripe pears, peeled   1 teaspoon lemon juice
4 tablespoons honey   ground ginger
¼ cup chopped walnut meats

Remove the cores from the pears with an apple corer. Mix together in a bowl the honey, walnuts, lemon juice and a small pinch ginger. Put this stuffing inside the pears. Grease a baking pan, place on the bottom shelf of the oven and bake for 40 minutes at 400°F. Remove the lid from the pan 10 minutes before the end of the cooking time. Serve at once.

INDEX OF RECIPES